CASH FROM YOL

Other How To Books for Family Reference

Applying for Legal Aid
Arranging Insurance
Becoming a Father
Buying a Personal Computer
Choosing a Nursing Home
Choosing a Package Holiday
Dealing with a Death in the Family
How to Apply to an Industrial
  Tribunal
How to be a Local Councillor
How to be an Effective School
  Governor
How to Claim State Benefits
How to Lose Weight & Keep Fit
How to Make a Wedding Speech

How to Plan a Wedding
How to Raise Funds & Sponsorship
How to Run a Local Campaign
How to Run a Voluntary Group
How to Survive Divorce
How to Take Care of Your Heart
How to Use the Internet
Making a Complaint
Managing Your Personal Finances
Successful Grandparenting
Successful Single Parenting
Taking in Students
Teaching Someone to Drive
Winning Consumer Competitions

Other titles in preparation

The How To Series now contains more than 150 titles in the following categories:

Business Basics
Family Reference
Jobs & Careers
Living & Working Abroad
Student Handbooks
Successful Writing

Please send for a free copy of the latest catalogue for full details (see back cover for address).

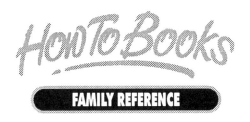

CASH FROM YOUR COMPUTER

How to sell word processing, book-keeping,
desktop publishing and other services

Zoe King

How To Books

Bol - 7610016y
KiN

Acknowledgements

My thanks must go to The National Back Pain Association for their invaluable help in the preparation of Chapter 1, and for permission to reproduce material from their literature. Thanks are also due to my husband David, for his unstinting help and support, particularly with Chapters 4 and 10, and to Roger Ferneyhough of How To Books for the guidance and encouragement he gave me.

331·7610016y

Cartoons by Mike Flanagan

British Library Cataloguing in Publication Data
A catalogue record for this book is available from the British Library.

First published in 1996 by How To Books Ltd, Plymbridge House, Estover Road, Plymouth PL6 7PZ, United Kingdom. Tel: (01752) 202301. Fax: (01752) 202331.

Note: The material contained in this book is set out in good faith for general guidance and no liability can be accepted for loss or expense incurred as a result of relying in particular circumstances on statements made in the book. The laws and regulations are complex and liable to change, and readers should check the current position with the relevant authorities before making personal arrangements.

Produced for How To Books by Deer Park Productions.

Typeset by Concept Communications, (Design & Print) Ltd, Crayford, Kent.
Printed and bound by Cromwell Press, Broughton Gifford, Melksham, Wiltshire.

Contents

List of Illustrations

Preface

If you are fortunate enough to own both a reasonably powerful personal computer and a high quality output printer, and are totally proficient in using them and their accompanying software, the amount of money you can make is limited only by the time you are prepared to spend at your computer.

Small companies, shops, charities, churches, health centres, leisure centres and many other organisations will welcome your offers to produce their newsletters, press releases, posters, accounts and so forth. As long as you have access to good word-processing, you can make money. If you also have access to database software, an accounting package, desk top publishing, or any of the other, more specialised programs around, you can make a great deal more.

If you *want* to make money using your home computer, you've taken the first step in buying this book. Now read on, and see how easy it can be . . .

Zoe King

1
Thinking about the Possibilities

WORKING FROM HOME – THE BENEFITS

As more and more people are beginning to realise, working from home has much to recommend it. The hardest part of going out to work is very often the getting there. Facing rush hour traffic and the worst that the weather can throw at you day after day is no joke. Indeed, it's a sad fact that going out to work can damage your health. Working from home, however, cuts out a great many of the stresses and strains.

Advantages versus disadvantages

Advantages
1. You don't have to 'go' anywhere. Technically, when you wake up, you're at work!

2. Less travelling cuts down considerably on stress. The travelling you *are* involved in should be paid for by your clients.

3. Overheads are minimal.

Disadvantages
1. Others have a tendency to assume that if you're working from home, you're 'fair game' for a cup of tea and a chat, or to deal with their problems.

2. You may need a strong sense of purpose and motivation to get down to work.

3. In winter, the house will need to be heated all day, rather than just morning and evening.

4. You may miss the normal cut and thrust of working with others.

The advantages speak for themselves. Let's look briefly at the disadvantages.

1. Stress to family and friends that you are not at home for their benefit, but, initially at least, for your own. Tell them you are starting a new venture, and you'd be grateful for their help and support, which includes them respecting the time when you are technically 'at work'.

2. Once you are confident enough to start work, motivation will come from the fact that there are people out there willing to pay you to work for them. To help you reach that stage, read on, and let the book act as your driving force.

3. Additional heating costs may well add to the household's financial burden, but you can offer to help meet the costs, because you *will* be earning.

4. You will be seeing other people, but on a different footing from before. Give yourself time to adjust; you'll soon find yourself too busy to miss your erstwhile colleagues.

LOOKING AT YOUR CURRENT ASSETS

The hardware

I am assuming that you already own your own **computer** (486 upwards with *at least* 4 mb of RAM and a 100+mb hard disk), together with a range of **software**, and a high quality output **printer** (preferably inkjet or laser). In addition, you almost certainly have access to a **telephone**. If you also have a **fax machine**, an **answering machine** and a **photo-copier**, so much the better. The fax machine will enable clients with their own machine to fax you details of their requirements. The answering machine should mean that you won't lose work when you are unable to answer the phone. And the photocopier? It's an added bonus, which might open the way for additional work, and thus income.

SETTING UP YOUR WORK STATION

Making it your own

The place in which you choose to work should be warm, comfortable and welcoming. It should also, as far as possible, be *yours*. Apart from any psychological need you may have to 'own' your work space, it is *absolutely essential* that the work you are doing for clients should be safeguarded from damage caused by other members of your household. If you cannot secure a room of your own, create a work space within a room, and make sure that everyone understands that this is your territory. You will, if you follow my advice, be storing incoming work in a filing cabinet, which should be kept locked when you are away from the house. Let the cabinet become your 'safe', where you'll keep all the tools of your trade, including the floppy disks on which you'll store your clients' work.

Looking after your back

The way you sit at your computer can decidedly affect the quality and quantity of your output. According to The National Back Pain Association, over two million people in Britain are chronically ill or disabled because of back pain, and the incidence is growing, particularly among sedentary workers. One of the principal causes is poor posture, caused in part by badly designed office seating, combined with poorly positioned computer screens.

How you should sit

You should use a properly designed office **chair** (see Figure 1) with adjustments for height and backrest. You should be able to sit with your feet flat on the floor, or on a footrest, particularly if you already suffer from lower back pain; unsupported feet can place more stress on the spine.

1. The operator's feet are flat on the floor, and there is plenty of room for her knees.
2. The seat backrest gives maximum support to the small of the back.
3. The seat itself is well padded, to ensure maximum comfort.
4. The chair has the recommended five-star base, for maximum stability.
5. Chair arms are optional. Some people cannot manage without them, others find them a hindrance.
6. The computer screen is directly in line with the operator's field of vision.

Fig. 1. The optimum position for you and your computer.

The **seat height** should be adjusted so that your keyboard is at, or just below, elbow height. The seat should be well padded and covered with non-slip fabric. The **backrest** should be adjusted to give the maximum amount of support to the small of the back. Finally, the chair should have a five-pointed star base, to give maximum stability, and should have castors only if it is on a carpeted floor.

Having dealt with your chair, consider the height of the desk and the computer screen. The **desk** should be high enough, with no intruding panels or drawers, to comfortably accommodate you with your chair in the optimum position. The **computer screen** should be placed so that you can look at it without bending or stretching your neck. If it is too low, raise the height with a board or book.

Finally, if you are involved in long stretches of work, take frequent **breaks**. Stand up and walk around the room, and stretch in several directions before returning to work.

The National Back Pain Association produces some excellent leaflets, including one specifically aimed at office workers, entitled *Better Backs for Office Workers*, which is free in return for a stamped addressed envelope (see Useful Addresses).

Being kind to your eyes

It is now well known that long periods spent in front of a computer screen can have significant effects on the eyes. The following are recommended guidelines for avoiding eye strain and headaches caused by screen glare:

● Your computer monitor should be at right angles to the window, so that the window is not reflected in it.

● Avoid fluorescent lights. They flicker, and cause screen reflections.

● Adjust the screen contrast to provide the minimum amount of glare.

● The use of an anti-glare screen filter can be beneficial.

● Try to ensure that the wall at the back of the monitor is a fairly neutral colour, so that you can rest your eyes occasionally by looking at it, rather than the monitor.

● Take frequent short breaks – ten minutes or so every two hours, at least.

One final word. Consider installing an **ioniser** in your office area. Computers produce positive ions, which can significantly affect your work rate because of their tendency to induce listlessness and headaches. An ioniser will correct this situation by restoring the balance of ions in the atmosphere, thus renewing your capacity for work.

Don't be tempted to skip setting up your office space correctly in favour of getting down to work without delay; attention paid to these points now will ensure that you don't suffer unnecessary health problems in the future.

THINKING ABOUT YOUR STORAGE SYSTEMS

Storing clients' work

You may have blanched at the idea of storing your clients' work on **floppy disks**, but let's think for a moment about the pros and cons of the alternative – storing on the computer's **hard disk**:

Pros

● It's easier; the disk is already in place, and you don't have to define it, you simply click on an icon, and the work is saved.

● It's quicker, and if you save automatically you lose less work time.

● The work is instantly accessible when you return to the computer after a break.

● You don't have to worry about storing and organising lots of floppy disks.

Cons

● Saving temporary files on the hard disk can create 'cluster' problems on the disk, which will then need to be de-fragmented if it is to work efficiently.

● The hard disk can become unnecessarily cluttered with large files, particularly when DTP work is stored.

● File names can become a problem where you are doing several tasks for one client.

● If the unthinkable happens, and the computer crashes, files may be lost.

Whilst the pros might seem very tempting, the cons should make it clear that saving onto floppies is far more sensible given the possible problems it solves. Cluster problems on the hard disk result when files are saved, then deleted; the software will then take longer to load, and your computer will be slower in operation. Also you may experience problems when trying to save work. Worst of all, the computer may take it into its head to 'crash', which means that you will be taken out of the program into an error message. If this happens, you will definitely lose any unsaved work, and may lose other files, depending upon the severity of the crash. The only way to solve these problems is to 'de-frag' the disk in order to tidy it up; a process which can take several hours, and rob you of working time.

Naming your files

The question of file names is one which exercises even the most able brains. Unless you use Windows '95, you will know that you are restricted to eight letters, wherever you save your files. Floppy disk savers who use a separate floppy for each client can physically label the disk with both the client's name and the file names, whereas hard disk savers are restricted to one eight letter word. Experience shows that, given the way most minds work, tasks of the same kind tend to produce similar file names, creating endless confusion. If you save onto floppies, you can use a dual system of labelling files. Finally, and probably most importantly, you have an instant 'back-up' copy of all current work should the computer crash.

Devising your systems

In order to avoid confusion, and to make access to your clients' work as efficient as possible, you must devise a shorthand which enables instant recognition of the work in hand.

Suppose you are word-processing college assignments for a student named Ellis, an English student who is writing about Thomas Hardy and Wilfred Owen.

Mr Ellis's floppy disk will be physically labelled 'Ellis' using one of the labels provided by the disk manufacturer. (Incidentally, when using these labels, make *absolutely sure* that they stick firmly to the disk, as disk drive damage can result from a peeling label. For this reason, it is not a good idea to store spare labels, as the adhesive can quite quickly deteriorate.)

You might be tempted to name Mr Ellis's assignments 'A', 'B', 'C', but you'll have no way of knowing which is which. Use shorthand versions of the title and/or author names to create a file name. In our two examples, the Hardy might be called simply 'Hardy' and the Owen 'Owen'. However, if Mr Ellis presented you with two essays about Hardy, you would need to devise a shorthand based upon the title. *Far from the Madding Crowd* might become 'Hardyfar', for example, and *Tess of the Durbervilles* 'Hardytes'. Remember, you are restricted to eight letters, so you need to be inventive. Using that system in conjunction with a diary in which you record the requirements of each client, the due-by date, and what you are charging, should mean that you avoid possible confusion about what work you are doing for whom.

INSURING AGAINST DISASTER

'There's nowt so queer as computers' a friend used to say, particularly when they take it into their heads to crash, or lose your work, or alter the formatting, or whatever it happens to be. In order to minimise the effects of some of these computer quirks, get into the habit *now* of backing up the day's work. **Do it every evening**, before you switch the computer off.

Backing up is like an insurance policy: whatever happens, your work is safe. If you work in Windows, you should find a simple Microsoft Backup program which will 'talk' you through the process. If you work within DOS, read the manual to find the commands relating to your particular version. Either way, learn to back-up without delay, so that you save yourself a great deal of hassle should the worst happen.

Floppies versus tape streamer or external drive

Saving onto floppy disks kept specifically for the purpose is the way most of us deal with backing-up. The disks are cheap, and are, with the occasional exception, reliable. It could be argued, however, that where you have a large volume of work to back-up, using floppies is a time consuming process which keeps the computer out of action for too long. The solution could be to invest in a tape streamer, a small unit which either sits outside the processor box, or, more conveniently, fits into a spare disk drive bay. A tape streamer uses mini cassettes to back up the day's work, and will back up large amounts of data in a very short time. They are relatively inexpensive given their efficiency, and might be worth considering if you find yourself involved with large volumes of work at any one time. Another possible solution could be the use of an additional external hard drive, or one of the new 'Zip' drives, but both of these would prove considerably more expensive.

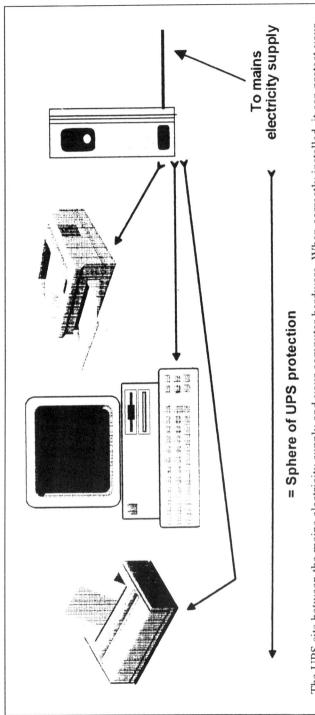

To mains electricity supply

= Sphere of UPS protection

Fig. 2. The UPS.

The UPS sits between the mains electricity supply and your computer hardware. When correctly installed, it can protect your computers, printers and peripheral equipment, and will allow your printer to finish a printing job without loss of work.

Installing a UPS unit

An Uninterruptable Power Supply (UPS) unit is the one piece of additional equipment which you really cannot afford to be without if you work in an area subject to peaks and troughs of electricity supply. The unit, a small box-like affair, sits between your computer and printer, and the source of power supplying both, and protects your hardware from sudden electricity breakdowns (see Figure 2). If your electric power fails, the UPS takes over for 15 minutes or so, giving you sufficient time to save your work, and power down your computer. The better models also iron out any peaks and troughs of supply which occur.

How does it work?

The UPS is, in effect, a rechargeable battery unit, which is kept on optimum charge by being connected to your electricity supply. That way, it is always ready for use should the worst happen. When the electricity fails, the unit takes over. Should you not be at your desk when that happens, you will know the unit is working because it emits a repeated 'bleep' during the first 30 seconds or so of its operation. When the electricity supply is returned, the unit hands back the reins, and is recharged ready for next time. Once installed, your UPS unit will save your sanity many times, and will quickly repay its modest cost.

QUESTIONS AND ANSWERS

I'm not sure I've enough confidence to approach people for work. What if they all say 'No'?

Don't worry about that at the moment. When the time comes, other chapters in the book will talk you through the best methods of approach. When you do come to 'asking' for work, as you put it, you'll be selling your expertise, not yourself. If you have confidence in your own ability to do the work, that will be enough to persuade potential clients that you fit the bill. As for them all saying 'no', if you follow my guidelines, enough will say 'yes' to enable you to build up your confidence and your business.

I like the sound of the UPS unit, and the safeguards it offers, but do I really need to buy one before I set up in business?

No, nor do you 'need' to buy many of the other expensive items I mention. I would suggest that you leave relatively major purchases until you are sure you are going to make a go of working for yourself. By that time, you will have accumulated enough money in the bank to be able to justify their purchase on the grounds that they are going to make your operations more professional and efficient.

You mention that long periods spent working on computers can have significant effects on the eyes. I already wear spectacles for close work: should I expect my eyes to worsen once I start work?
No. The negative effects can be largely avoided by following the guidelines set out. Have your eyes tested as recommended by your optician, and if there is any significant deterioration in your condition, ask him for guidance.

CASE STUDIES

Let us now take a look at three computer owners whose progress we will be following in the succeeding chapters. Each comes from a different background, and has his or her own speciality, which affects their approach to using their computer to make money.

Brian Woods, retired accountant
Brian Woods BA FCCA was the chief accountant of a large financial services company until company restructuring forced his early retirement. Whilst he is enjoying the freedom his retirement offers, he realises that at 54 he is capable of using his skills to earn sufficient money to considerably enhance his company pension. Brian has always been a self starter, has a good education and is always ready to accept a challenge. His staff regarded him as a good and approachable manager, and he feels his varied experience with the company should stand him in good stead when it comes to offering his services on a self-employed basis.

Andrew Lloyd, mature student awaiting university placement
Andrew Lloyd (23) grew up with computers and had hoped that his interest would lead to a lucrative post in the computer industry. However, after studying the technical side of computer hardware for several years, he realised that he was dissatisfied in this field, as it did not give vent to his considerable design skills. After taking an Access course at his local college, he applied to several universities for placement on an art and design course. Andrew is a good all-rounder, technically competent and very skilled at DTP layout. He sees his word-processing skills as a necessary evil, but is well aware of the potential both they and his computer skills offer.

Alison Davies, freelance writer

Alison Davies (35) has worked as a fairly casual freelance writer since her youngest child went to school. Although writing brings in the occasional financial reward, Alison feels that she needs something which will bring in a steadier income, given her single parent status. Before marriage, Alison worked in various posts, and has fairly wide secretarial skills, which she has kept up through voluntary work in the community. She is a frustrated artist and enjoys DTP and design, although writing offers little scope for development in that field. She would like to branch out in order to expand her knowledge and her chances of earning a regular income.

2
Breaking into Word Processing

GETTING STARTED

When you are satisfied that your chosen workplace is set up with due regard to both comfort and health, and that it will not be subject to the sticky fingers or muddy paws of other members of your family, you can seriously consider offering a word-processing service. However, in order to make your entry into word-processing as organised and trouble-free as possible, you should first ensure that you are properly equipped.

THINKING ABOUT SUPPLIES

Before you start, you will need to think about **paper**. Paper for office use comes in a bewildering range of grades, weights and finishes, as a glance at a commercial office supplier's catalogue will reveal. In order to produce work of the required quality, you will need to know which papers are suited to which tasks. There are papers which advertise themselves as 'all purpose', and which claim they are suitable for most office tasks, but in practice they do not offer the finished result which most of your clients will be looking for.

In practice, when starting out you probably need to buy only two grades of paper. Your first requirement is a high quality bond (with matching envelopes) which you will use for headed notepaper for your own use, formal letters for your clients, and some of your finished output. The second is an 80gsm copier or inkjet paper (depending upon which sort of printer you use), which you will use for draft copies and/or finished output where the quality of paper is less important. The crucial thing to remember about paper qualities is that high grades cost considerably more than their lower grade counterparts, and must be costed out accordingly. The client who insists upon the finest paper must understand that he will pay for the privilege.

Buying your paper

Having decided upon the types of paper you want, you must then think about **suppliers**. Try to avoid the temptation of buying small quantities from a local shop. Buying this way will add considerably to your costs, and thus to your charges to your clients. The *only* way to buy paper is to buy by the ream (usually 500 sheets). Most mail order office suppliers offer generous discounts on multiple purchases, so it would be wise to consider buying the less expensive paper in larger quantities if you can afford it, as this is the paper you will use most often.

Cutting delivery costs
The more expensive paper is less likely to be offered at a bulk discount, but it might still be wiser to buy two or three packs, if doing so will cut down on your carriage costs. Some suppliers offer free carriage if your order exceeds a certain minimum cost, so it makes sense to order all your requirements at one time, rather than in bits and pieces. Viking Direct, for instance, currently offers free carriage on orders over £30.00, and promises a next day delivery service where orders are placed early in the day. They also offer 30 day terms to customers who have pre-paid one or two orders, which means that you should be able to manage your cash flow more efficiently (see Useful Addresses).

Obtaining other supplies
Having dealt with your first and perhaps most important requirement, you must now think about other supplies. You will need bulk supplies of floppy disks, and spares of inkjet cartridges, printer ribbons, and so forth. All of these items should be available from your office supplier. It goes without saying that if you are to be seen as a professional, you must *never* find yourself in the position of having to hold up a client's work because you have run out of basic essentials.

Finally, you should think about obtaining a good **dictionary** if you don't own one already. The two volume *Shorter Oxford* offers a comprehensive overview of current English at a reasonable price, and is probably the minimum you will require. Whilst you may imagine you can depend upon your word processor's own dictionary, you will soon realise that it is not nearly sophisticated enough, particularly when you start doing specialised work.

Storing hard copies
The efficient storage of hard copies, *ie* paper copies, of work in progress will be best met by the use of a small **filing cabinet**. Most of your clients, particularly students, are likely to give you hand-written notes from which to work. You will also need to print out first and subsequent drafts of some work, which will be sent off to your clients for their

Paper type	Weight or grade	Suggested uses	Comments
Listing	60-80gsm[1], perforated, tractor fed	Useful for accounting output, draft *etc* on dot matrix printers.	Generally poor quality, but can save money where good paper is not essential.
Bond, *eg* 'Conqueror'	100gsm 'laid' or 'wove'	High quality output, CVs, letters, DTP output on laser or inkjet.	Comes in several colours, expensive, but worth the extra outlay where quality is paramount.
'Copier'	70-80gsm 'smooth' white	Photocopying, 1st drafts on dot matrix or laser printers.	Cheap and cheerful, 1/4 price of bond, useful for many different tasks, but too absorbent for inkjet printing unless specifically modified.
'Colour copier'	80gsm 'smooth' colours	Designed specifically for copiers, but invaluable for DTP output, notices, newsletter covers *etc*. Anywhere where you want to attract attention.	Usually more expensive than white, but useful where you want to attract attention.
'Copier card'	160gsm white and colours	Document covers, notices, file dividers, invitations *etc*.	Comes in a wide variety of colours, more durable than paper, but approximately twice the price. Usually supplied in 250 sheet packs.
Bank	45-50gsm, white and colours	Useful where multiple carbon copies are required by dot matrix printer users.	Lightweight and relatively inexpensive, but more often used by typists.
Inkjet	80-100gsm	Inkjet printing.	Treated surface promises high resolution copies. Medium priced.
Laser	90-100gsm	Laser printer use.	Manufactured to withstand high temperatures met in laser printers.
Premium laser	100gsm	High opacity for double sided and high dpi[2] 'camera ready' output.	Very expensive; worth buying only for specific jobs.

1. 'gsm' = grammes per square metre. Papers of 70gsm and under are considered lightweight, and not suitable for finished output. 80-90 gsm is general purpose paper. 100gsm is high quality. Many printers will not accept papers above this weight, although modern photocopiers will often accept heavier papers and card.

2. 'dpi' = dots per inch, which refers to the quality of output from various printers. The higher the dpi figure, the finer the resolution.

Fig. 3. The various grades of paper available.

comments and corrections. Simple hanging files, labelled with each client's name, will ensure the safe and efficient storage of such papers.

Buying second-hand
Filing cabinets come in various sizes, and you'll find that most office stationery suppliers can offer new models fairly cheaply. However, you might do better to search the 'Office Supplies' columns of your local newspaper to see if you can find a second hand model. If you are lucky, make sure that all the drawers open smoothly, and that the runners have not been damaged. With most filing cabinets, previous rough handling shows up here. When you go to collect your cabinet, ask if you can buy some of the hanging files which fitted into the filing drawers. If not, look out for packs of ten or twelve files, aimed at home users. Shop around for the best price, but don't sacrifice quality for cheapness, as your files will have to withstand a fair amount of wear and tear.

FINDING YOUR FIRST CLIENTS

Have you ever stopped to consider how you would manage without your computer? Just think of all those laborious hours spent writing letters, essays and articles by hand or typewriter. *That's* how students feel. It's no joke writing 8,000 – 10,000 word essays by hand. As ex-students will know, essays are not written out just once, they are written out several times – firstly in draft form, then in revised draft, and finally in presentation form. In addition, there may well be lots more writing in between. So, the poor old student is an ideal starting point for your word-processing business, particularly as more and more colleges and universities are insisting that final drafts of essays, projects and assignments *must* be typed or word-processed.

Advertising for student clients
To find your student clients, contact the Students Unions of local colleges or universities and ask how you go about advertising on their notice boards. Generally, you will be able to advertise your services free, but you may find some Unions charge a small flat fee per week or month. Hunt around for the most cost-effective opportunities, and take advantage of them. Also, leave your name and details with the people in the Administration Office of the same establishments, as academic staff are often glad of word-processing services.

Designing your advertisement
When drafting your advertisement, don't simply throw together a few

Word Processing . . . Word Processing . . . Word Processing

Did someone mention "Word Processing"?

Yes, I did, and I can offer *special rates* for students

From just £3.00 per thousand words!

All work spell checked, grammar checked,
collected, and delivered.

Call Alison on 0151 609 3456

Fig. 4. An effective small advertisement. Note the use of white space,
and different sizes of text, used together with italics, to draw
attention to the wording.

lines, offering word-processing at cheap rates. If your ad looks cheap
and cheerful, that will tell those seeing it something about the quality of
your work. Instead, draft a carefully worded and designed ad, using the
skills you hope to sell, and rather than simply quoting a lower rate than
other advertisers, offer a special rate for students only. That way, if your
ad attracts the attentions of academic staff, you'll be able to charge *them*
the going rate.

Setting rates for your work
When setting your rates, remember the magic word 'from', so that you
can adjust your charges where a client asks for better quality paper or
extra copies.

Spelling it out
Once you start work, you'll be gaining lots of invaluable experience
about what people want out of a word-processing service, and how best
to meet their needs. A word of caution here: when working for students,
you may well find that you are faced with lots of specialised terminology, which you've never met before and certainly cannot spell. It's a good
idea to ask your students to write such words in block letters, because
the chances are they won't appear in your newly acquired dictionary.
Next, take a few moments to discuss format. Most colleges and universities have fairly set rules about how work should be presented. Make

sure you fully understand their requirements. Discuss the level of print-out required: is this a first or revised draft, or is it the final polished product? The answer will determine the quality of paper used.

Finally, make sure that you have a telephone number where you can contact your client in the event of any confusion. That way, you don't lose valuable time trekking backwards and forwards seeking an opinion on a word or group of words.

PUTTING A PRICE ON YOUR SKILLS AND TIME

Putting a price on your skills and time may seem to be simply a matter of charging per thousand words, and for the most part it will be. But there will always be work which requires more time and expertise, and you must remember to **charge accordingly** if you are not to be seen as someone to be taken advantage of. Page after page of text should be charged at the going rate, but consider the chart in Figure 5.

Supposing your client asks you to reproduce charts similar to those in Figure 5. How long do you think it might take you? Many top-end pack-ages could produce it without difficulty, but it will inevitably take longer than producing straight text. You may imagine that you can comfortably charge the usual rate, and with just one or two such charts, you probably

Proportion of population under 35 yrs who have experienced homelessness during last five years

Fig. 5. The kind of chart you might be asked to produce.

could, but before you quote your rate for the job, make absolutely sure that your client doesn't have several dozen of these up his sleeve. Look carefully at the work involved *before* you quote, and if you are not sure how long a certain section might take you, say so, and let your client know that you may have to charge slightly more, depending upon the time taken.

Exploiting your potential

Never undersell yourself, but at the same time, if you *do* find you can produce the goods in the optimum time, thanks to the sophistication of your word-processing package, let your client know, so that he can spread the word about your specialist potential. That way, you may be given work that others are not capable of carrying out.

CHECKING CLIENT REQUIREMENTS

When you first meet potential clients and talk over their requirements, make *absolutely sure* that you know what kind of output they require. The kind of questions you need to ask are:

- what paragraph styles you should use

- style and size of typeface

- quality of paper

- how many copies, and of what quality, *ie* draft, final draft

- any special requirements, for example specialist characters, which you may not be able to reproduce (particularly important with mathematics and science students)

- any 'hard words', such as technical or jargon expressions

- to edit or not to edit

- the date the work is required.

Formatting the work
Paragraph styles will vary according to the type of work involved. Make sure you **fully understand** your client's requirements.

Typefaces for straightforward text are generally fairly limited. For the most part, use either Times Roman, or a sans serif typeface such as

Helvetica or Arial, and stick to 11 or 12 point unless your client advises otherwise. However, when you find yourself doing anything even slight-ly out of the ordinary, discuss the possibility of using other, fancier, typefaces, to liven up the appearance of the work. Take along samples of work produced using the fonts to which you have access.

Deciding on paper
The quality of paper required will depend upon the final destination of the output. First and second drafts will often be on cheaper grades of paper, but final drafts invariably look much more impressive on good paper. Talk to your client about the different grades of paper you can offer. Show him samples and let him decide, but remember to cost out the extra expense of using better grades.

Charging for extra copies
Where you have to provide more than one copy of work, charge accord-ingly. If you have access to a photocopier you can make copies quickly and easily, at minimal cost, but if you have to print out several copies of a long and complex document, you will add considerably to your costs, particularly where you are using good paper.

Accepting specialised work
Special requirements might mean charts and graphs, drawings, equa-tions, mathematical formulae, or in fact almost anything! Before accept-ing such work, make absolutely sure that your system is capable of pro-ducing it. Do you have access to mathematical character sets for instance? Could you reproduce the following?

$$\int_a^b f(x)dx = \lim \frac{b-a}{n} \sum_{r=1}^{n} \left(a + \frac{r}{n}(b-a) \right)$$

Thank heavens you don't need to know what it all means, but you may need to reproduce it when working for a mathematics or science student or tutor.

Understanding jargon
'Hard' or jargon words can present particular difficulties. Remember to ask your client to write then out in CAPITAL letters. Don't imagine that you'll simply remember them, or that you can look them up in your dictionary; specialist and/or jargon words are often not reproduced in dictionaries as they are not in general usage. Psychological and socio-logical language, for instance, changes quite quickly, so that even

specialist dictionaries may not contain some words. Save yourself valuable time by checking before you leave.

Deciding whether to edit
As to the thorny question of whether or not to edit a student's (or tutor's) work: whilst you can be fairly confident about correcting obvious howlers, you may find what you consider to be their rather idiosyncratic way of writing is considered by them to be perfect prose. **Do not** edit without their express permission. If you do, you risk causing offence.

Noting the deadline for return of work
Having ascertained the date the work is required, make a note in your work diary, and also place a header on the computer document, detailing the client's name and the due-by date. Use a different font colour for this note, so that you know it must be removed before the work is printed out.

EXPANDING YOUR OPERATIONS

It's worth considering several routes to expansion when you judge the time is right. You can advertise your services in the local press, or you might consider approaching local businesses direct. It's easy to imagine that most companies use computers in this day and age, and are unlikely to need your services, but this is far from true. A great many small shops, sole traders and small businesses have never even considered the idea that a computerised system would help them to run their businesses. This is where you come in.

Show, don't tell
Don't just assume that companies will welcome you with open arms the minute you make your suggestions. *Show* them how valuable you could be. Before you make your initial approach, learn a little about the business and do a dummy write-up of some sort. Lots of small traders would be glad of someone to produce advertising leaflets, economically produced letter heads, compliment slips, shopping vouchers and so forth. They won't approach printers because of the imagined cost, but will welcome *you* if you make it clear that you can produce what they want at a fraction of the cost of the local printer, who may well have huge overheads to consider. If you do decide to go down this road, keep your prices as low as you realistically can whilst still making a profit. Your initial profit margins may be low, but if the quality of your work is good, word will soon spread, and you may well find yourself with more work than you can cope with.

Producing newsletters

A very lucrative area for word processors is the production of **newsletters**. If you have access to a photocopier, you can produce *and* print newsletters for a variety of local concerns, such as charities, churches and leisure centres. The most effective way to ensure the interest of those approached is again to do some homework, then to present them with a sample of what you can do – preferably featuring *them*. All organisations benefit through keeping in touch with their members, and simply produced newsletters can do the job at minimal cost. As long as your charges are reasonable, you can talk yourself into a job.

If your intended clients produce a newsletter at the moment, get hold of a copy and produce the same thing yourself, but better and cheaper. Make full use of the graphics capabilities of your word processor to produce a professional looking job. If the newsletter has six pages, stick to six pages, but make every one of them count in terms of page design. This will often be sufficient in itself to persuade someone whose current output is a simple typewritten affair.

Talking to printers and copy shops

If you don't have access to a photocopier, approach local printers and copy shops and see if they will offer you a special deal in return for lots of work being put their way. Talk to as many as you can, and go for the cheapest, as long as his output is good. Persuade him to reduce his prices even further by offering to negotiate free advertising in some of the publications.

General advertising

An additional option for acquiring word-processing work is advertising in the local newspaper or specialist publication. This is tending to be a somewhat overloaded area, but may be worth a try if you consider that your locality is not well served. If you decide to advertise, don't simply fire off a few words, then sit back waiting for the telephone to ring. Think carefully about how your ad will be presented: a carefully worded and displayed ad will bring in more business than a few words stuck in the middle of all the other small ads. In order to attract customers, you must make them notice *you* in preference to the opposition.

Advertising yourself

The whole point of advertising is to sell yourself and your services. Advertising costs money, but carefully thought-out advertising can increase your returns considerably. Contact your target publication and ask about **display** or semi display ads. Ask about repeat costs. One ad *may* catch the eye of a potential client, and bring in a small amount of work, but a series of ads will establish you and your services much more effectively. When making up the ad, think carefully about the wording. Don't just put 'Word Processing' and hope that your potential clients will read the rest of the advertisement. Sell yourself! Look at Figure 6, which I spotted in a local paper some months ago. It certainly caught my eye – I bet it caught the eye of people needing the service too. Remember to stress that your service includes 'free' spell and grammar checking and word counting too if your software offers these options. (If it doesn't, shouldn't you think about upgrading?)

When discussing your repeat ads with the advertising manager of your chosen publication, ask about discounts for multiple entries. You should be able to place two ads per week for the next three or four weeks at a reduced rate with the proviso that should you be inundated with replies, later ads can be cancelled or postponed.

TURNING DOWN WORK

If as a result of your advertising, or other approaches, you find you have

**You're wasting
your time
reading this**
if you can do your own
word processing.
**But if you can't,
why not talk to me?**

I can produce professional quality
documents, spell and
grammar checked,
at *very* reasonable rates.
Oh, and I'll even collect and
deliver locally . . .
Call me on ***********

Susan Ewart

Fig. 6. Another effective advertisement.

more work than you can cope with, *don't* be tempted to send out work which is not up to your usual standard, whilst continuing to take on more. If you do, you may find you lose business. It is far wiser to explain to would-be clients that on this occasion you must refuse the work, but that you'd be happy to work for them in the future. However, if one of your regular clients turns up with work which he needs 'yesterday', and you have work in hand which is required next week, accept the new task and charge accordingly.

Reviewing your charges

When you find yourself with more work than you can cope with, it is time to consider reviewing your charges. Putting them up a little will perhaps deter some potential clients, but those who have become accustomed to your high standards will stay with you.

CHECKLIST

- Check out local and mail order suppliers of stationery supplies, and place your initial order with due regard to available storage space, quantity discount, and carriage charges.

- Think carefully about storing work, and devise your own fool-proof filenames system.

- Remember to check your client's requirements carefully, and don't take on work which you cannot cope with.

- When you advertise, make the ad work for you. Remember, advertising costs money: you must see a return on your investment.

CASE STUDIES

Brian's first approach

Brian Woods decided that he could improve his word-processing speed and accuracy by taking on a limited amount of fairly undemanding work. He placed several small lineage ads in the local paper offering his services under an assumed company name. Even though he undercut the charges of other advertisers, few people contacted him, and of those who did, only one, a local freelance writer, required work that he could cope with. Brian concluded that the advertisement wording was to blame for the lack of response, and decided that next time he would pay slightly more in order to increase the response rate, and thus his options.

Andrew goes back to college

Andrew Lloyd decided that the best starting point for him would be his old college. He persuaded his friend Simon, who was in charge of the Union notice boards, to allow him to advertise without charge. He placed ads on several notice boards, and was soon inundated with work.

However, he discovered quite early that his student friends were more than ready to take advantage of their friendship with him, and he had considerable difficulty in extracting money from some of them. Others would try to beat him down on his £ per 1000 word rate. He concluded that perhaps his 'friends' were not, after all, the ideal starting point, and decided to offer his services in another part of the college, a strategy which brought him less work, but from more financially reliable sources.

Alison plays the field

Alison Davies decided to put a toe in the water by contacting local organisations. She was already doing a small amount of voluntary word-processing and DTP work for a local charity, and was able to use her contacts to obtain more work. She also advertised at the local FE college, obtaining a considerable amount of work. However, on reflection, she felt she had been wrong to advertise free collection and delivery at her student rate because of the time and extra expense involved. She was agreeably surprised by the amount of work she was able to complete, and was pleased to see how much she was earning as a result of her early approaches. However, she also realised that, unless she paid to keep her ads on the boards on a fairly permanent basis, work soon trailed off as assignments were completed.

DISCUSSION POINTS

1. Draw up a list of local sole traders, small businesses and charitable organisations which you might approach. What sort of dummies might you most usefully produce for perhaps half a dozen of them?

2. Buy several issues of your local newspaper and study the wording of some of the ads. If you were in the market for the advertised services, which ads would tempt you to reply, and why?

3. Does your word-processing program incorporate mathematical symbols or equations? Does it include a drawing package? How many of these special features have you explored?

3
Helping Others Find Work

PRODUCING CVs

In today's job market, competition for jobs is *very* fierce. Particularly where executive posts are concerned, applicants don't get a second chance to make a good first impression; those who impress from the start with an impeccably produced CV (curriculum vitae) are those who will go forward for interview. This is where you and your computer come in. However, before you can offer this service, you need to be aware of the different kinds of CV and the way in which they are produced.

General versus specific

General purpose CVs are produced for applicants who wish to apply for many jobs, and who are happy not to slant their application for each particular job. These CVs are usually accompanied by a letter from the applicant which states his or her qualifications for the specific post applied for. You can produce these generalised CVs relatively easily, after your client has completed a suitably worded form, which you'll use in conjunction with a telephone call. They do not cost a lot to produce, and you won't make very much money from them unless you also take on the responsibility of producing the letters which accompany them.

However, CVs are increasingly being produced which are *specifically aimed* at selected appointments. This means that fairly prolonged discussion with the client is needed in order that the information reproduced on the CV is accurate and is suitably geared towards the desired position. Although I would argue that face-to-face interviewing is the *only* way to produce an executive CV, it may be possible, where circumstances prevent face-to-face contact, to replace interviewing with careful form filling, combined with telephone interviewing, to give you a broader picture of the applicant.

Finding your clients

By far the simplest way to contact potential clients is to place a series of

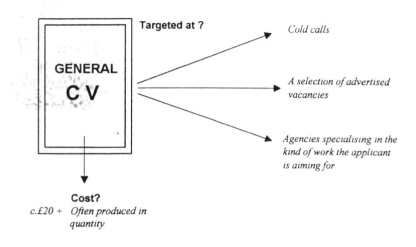

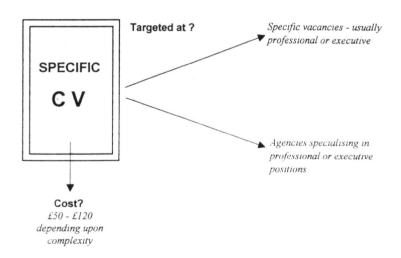

Fig. 7. General versus specific CVs.

advertisements in the local press. Choose the day(s) on which the paper runs its main job market pages, and insert your advertisement at the head of the job vacancies section. If you cannot afford display or semi display advertising, devise wording which starts with 'A', in order to get your ad in at the top of the column. Follow the guidelines set out earlier for successful advertising, making sure that your ad creates the impression of an expert in the field.

LOOKING AT GENERAL PURPOSE CVS

The idea of a CV is to give a potential employer a run-down of an applicant's previous education and experience. Based upon the given information, the employer will make the decision whether or not to spend valuable time interviewing the applicant. It follows therefore, that what goes into a CV is of vital importance. First and foremost, the employer wants to know whether or not the applicant is the best person for the job. Thus the kind of information which must be included is that which has a *direct* bearing upon the vacancies applied for.

There follows an example of a general purpose CV which could be used for a variety of applications. This kind of CV can be reproduced in quantity, and used for speculative approaches (*ie* the kind of application which says 'have you any vacancies for . . .?') as well as for actual advertised vacancies. Note that the information contained is fairly wide ranging, the idea being that many areas of expertise are mentioned, in the hope that one or more will appeal to the prospective employers contacted.

Deciding upon content

The aim in any CV must be to present a person who is capable and versatile, with a number of areas of expertise. Note that on Helen's CV (Figure 8), her educational qualifications take second place to her work experience, and her current position appears first. Fresh experience will undoubtedly be of more interest to potential employers than that gained in earlier positions. Also notice the personal information given. The fact that Helen is married might make her appear to be a more settled person than if she were footloose and fancy free. (Conversely, for some jobs, particularly those requiring long periods away from home, the absence of personal ties might make her a much more attractive bet.)

There are several things to notice about Helen's CV. First of all, it stretches to two pages. Although it could have been squeezed onto one page, the spacing around the entries makes them easy to read. Fighting to extract meaning from close text can be difficult, particularly where

Curriculum Vitae

HELEN ANDERSON

13 Charter's Walk
Leiston
Suffolk
01248 987654

Profile
A personal secretary/assistant of considerable experience,
with excellent communication skills and proven ability in all
office practice, including computer systems.

Career History

1990-Present   <u>Nuclear Electric</u>
PA to General Manager, Personnel and
Training Dept.
- Liaison with senior management.
- Arrangement of interviews, and carrying out
  preliminary interviewing at all levels.
- Day to day supervision of eight staff.
- Organisation of training schedules and course
  content in consultation with departmental
  management.

1983-1990   <u>Key Components Limited</u>
PA to Administration Manager
- Day to day supervision of six staff.
- Organisation of services to all departments.
- Liaison with outside suppliers.

1979-1983   <u>Inland Revenue South East</u>
Senior Executive Officer
General clerical duties, rose from Executive
Officer to SEO.

Fig. 8. A sample general purpose CV.

Education/Qualifications

1972-1979   Ipswich High School – 3 A-Level passes including English, 7 O-Level passes including mathematics and English.

Training

1990-Present   Diploma in Training and Development (ITD) (1992)
Various in-house courses including Personnel Management, (IPM based), DTP Design and Publishing, Spreadsheet management.

1983-1990   Training in PBX Switchboard operation, RSA Word Processing, Stages 1, 2, and 3, Shorthand Stages 1 & 2, and Book-keeping, Stages 1 & 2.

References

Anthony Lambert, B A, I P M   Mrs Janice Alder
The Lawns   47 The Street
Exton   Cambridge
Norfolk NR21 3GH   CB1 4DE

Hobbies and Interests

Classical music, gardening, bird watching, reading, mainly non-fiction.

Personal details

Date of birth: 8 November 1960.
Marital status: Happily married, no children.
Clean driving licence held for 10 years.

Fig. 8. A sample general purpose CV cont.

time is at a premium; far better to retain the spacing and take the information onto a second page. Also, notice the layout. The use of bullet points and indentations, together with bold type and underlining, makes the whole thing easy to read and assimilate. However, although space on the page is important, never be tempted to create CVs which run to more than two pages. Research has shown that the average time spent reading a CV amounts to no more than 1.5 minutes, which means anything vital on a third page is likely to be ignored.

Showing peripheral information

The most important details about Helen are her work experience and skills. Less important are the fact that she is N years old, and that she is married, with or without children. Her hobbies and interests have been mentioned, but briefly. If the interviewer wishes to know more, he or she will ask at the interview stage. Helen's CV makes no mention of why she left her various employers, or of the level of salary she is used to. If either of these aspects are considered important, they can be raised at interview; they have no place on either a general purpose or an executive CV.

OBTAINING THE INFORMATION

The most useful way to obtain the information for general CVs is to devise a **Personal Profile** form which asks for personal and educational information and previous work experience in full detail, which the client is asked to complete. The form can be used in conjunction with the telephone of course – any inconsistencies which arise can be dealt with via a quick phone call. It goes without saying that your clients must be assured of *absolute* confidentiality in their dealings with you, and the form should make that clear. Although the CV itself should never run to more than two pages, the form supplying the information should allow plenty of space, so that your client is encouraged to give as much information as possible.

These CVs should be run off on good quality 85–100 gsm paper, and the client provided with sheets of the same paper on which to write the application letter. If you choose to provide matching envelopes, you should charge accordingly. You should also agree at the outset how many copies of the CV will be included in the initial charge, and what you will charge for additional copies. It is usual with this kind of CV to give 10 or 12 copies, with extras being charged at a nominal rate of perhaps £2.00 – £3.00 per dozen.

WORKING IN THE EXECUTIVE MARKET

Producing CVs for the professional or executive is considerably more demanding than producing general purpose CVs. For every out-of-work executive you encounter, there are several dozen others, and the chances are that every job for which they apply will require a specialised application.

Interviewing your client

In order to get the best out of your potential client, and thus to produce the most effective CV, a face-to-face interview is virtually essential. Ideally, the interview should be taped, but if you cannot manage that, take copious notes, and/or ask your client to complete a *detailed* Personal Profile form. However, at this level, that is only half the work.

The skill in presenting your client to a potential employer lies in evaluating experience so far, and co-ordinating it with the requirements of the post applied for. Make sure you have a full picture of the job description for which the CV is aimed. Go carefully through the client's employment history, and tie in *any* potentially useful experience. Emphasise any strengths and understate any weaknesses. If for instance, your client is applying for a post as company accountant in a publishing corporation, and you notice he had experience as a book buyer some years ago, mention the fact. As a book buyer he will have been in close contact with publisher's representatives, and may well have been involved in publicity events and conferences. Enable your client to *sell* himself, so that between you, you convince the person on the receiving end of the CV that here is a serious contender for the position.

Presenting the information

When you are satisfied with the wording of the CV, you have to think carefully about **presentation**. For what sort of company is your client preparing his application? Is it a staid and respectable business house, or a young and thrusting advertising agency? The first would like to see a formally prepared CV, printed on finest quality 100 gsm paper, off-white or cream, with matching envelope. The second would probably be more impressed by something a little more adventurous – particularly if the vacancy is for a sales position.

Think about **layout**. Think about the fonts to which you have access – could you profitably use a slightly different one to draw attention towards the applicant? What about coloured paper? Could you perhaps choose a colour which you don't normally offer? It should still be finest quality of course, with matching envelope, but the fact that your client has clearly thought about his presentation will not be lost on the potential employer. As long as you are not too outrageous, you'll be able to use whatever paper you buy for another client, so don't be afraid to spend a little extra in order to give *this* client what he *really* wants.

Looking at an example of a specific CV
Figure 9 shows a CV produced for one John Appleby, who is applying for a position with a large multi-national company. The company has advertised for a Chief Accountant, who is capable of designing a new computerised system as well as overseeing all aspects of the company's accounting function. In addition to the need to emphasise what he sees as relevant experience, Mr Appleby is aware that his application should reflect the company's projected image, which is rather stuffy and high class. To that end, he has chosen off-white 'Conqueror' laid paper, which will be accompanied by a hand-written letter on the same paper. Recent research has shown that a hand-written covering letter is important in demonstrating an applicant's genuine interest in a particular job, given that word processors are so widely available.

When looking at the example, note the structure of the CV. The 'Profile' and 'Skills Analysis' sections give the potential employer an immediate impression of the applicant. These are followed by a breakdown of the applicant's career to date, with far more emphasis being placed upon recent experience, although the whole section should display progression of achievement and expertise. Note the use of the third person in the CV, rather than the first. This usage is now established practice, and has the effect of offering a more distanced and thus apparently more objective assessment.

QUESTIONS AND ANSWERS

Styles in CVs seem to vary so much, depending upon which guide you read. How will I know what sort to produce for each client?
The important thing to remember about CVs is that there are no hard and fast rules; there are as many styles and presentations as there are people reading them. By all means consult a good book which details the varying types, but be guided by the specific needs of your client, particularly when working in the executive market.

How should I respond to people replying to my advertisement? I don't want to spend hours on the telephone talking about the services I offer.
I would suggest that you create a professional looking information pack, which details the various services you are able to offer and your price

structure. Include a sample CV of a mythical person, printed on the kind of paper you will use for real CVs, and also the Personal Profile form, so that your client can get straight down to business. In order to create a good impression, produce your information packs before you place the ad so that you can send them out to potential clients immediately.

I've heard that some large organisations now use computers to 'read' CVs sent in response to professional journal advertisements, and that the computers are programmed to respond only to those CVs which include certain words. How can I possibly know which words to include?

This isn't as scary as it sounds. The practice is becoming more and more widespread in the executive field, but as long as you look carefully at the target recruitment advertisement, you should be fine. For the most part, the computer will be looking for those words which the advertisement has indicated are specific requirements for the job. So, if an ads says 'only graduates need apply', make sure you include the word 'graduate', or the letters which refer to the degree, *eg* BA, MA, or similar. If it asks for recently qualified accountants, make sure you insert the professional qualification in question. It is really only a matter of following the usual rules of CV compilation.

SETTING THE FEES

Charges for CVs vary enormously. The average in the South East is from around £20 for a non-specific CV to as much as £120 for a specifically targeted professional/executive CV. (CVs at this level are sometimes bound, which adds further to their cost.) Check out the position in your area by telephoning those firms advertising locally. Try to pitch your charges somewhere in between those already existing, but *don't* be tempted to charge less than recognised agencies charge for the service. If you do, you may well find that professional people will not approach you because they assume from your charges that your product will not be up to scratch.

Charging for amended repeats

If, in spite of your best efforts, your client is not successful in his application and would like you to produce another CV, with slightly different emphases, I would suggest you charge only a nominal sum, unless you are involved in considerable work. It goes without saying that all CVs should be saved onto a floppy, which should be filed and kept for a minimum of two years.

CURRICULUM VITAE

John R E M Appleby, BSc (Econ) FCCA
The Grange
Hr. Bebington
Wirral
Cheshire

Profile

A fully experienced, well motivated, senior accountant, used to communicating at the highest level, and reporting to the Finance Director. He is accustomed to working to strict timetables and deadlines, has exceptional PC skills, and is currently President of the district society of the ACCA, where he has been responsible for increasing active membership by some 50%.

Skills Analysis

- Responsible for overall accounting function
- Fully computer literate
- Successful formulation of long term strategy
- Excellent communication and interpersonal skills
- Wide experience of dealing with overseas clients
- Fluency in French and German, working knowledge of Italian

Employment History

1985-Date **Primor Research Limited, Chester**
Group Chief Accountant, responsible for overall accounting function, UK and Europe. Reporting to Finance Director.
Specialist in integral multi-tasking computer system design. Recent silver award winner: U.K. Corporate Function Design awards.

1980-1985 **F G Bramald (Certified Accountants)**
Bromborough, Cheshire
Tax Partner. Successfully implemented changeover to computer based system.

1974-1980 **Walker and Closs (Certified Accountants)**
Sevenoaks, Kent
PA to Senior Tax Partner

Fig. 9. A sample job-specific CV.

1963-1974	**Foreman, Roberts and Partners (Chartered Accountants), London EC1** ACCA trained, (qualified 1969). Subsequently, audit manager, working chiefly in company audit.

Education/Qualifications

1964-1969	ACCA, as detailed above. FCCA status - 1974
1958-1962	Birmingham University BSc Econ. Economics and Political Science
1952-1958	Wirral Grammar School, Cheshire 9 O-Levels, including Mathematics, English Language, Sciences, History, French and German 3 A-Levels – English, Mathematics, Modern Languages

Personal details

Date and place of birth:	06.06.40 Chester, Cheshire.
Home telephone no.	0151 608 29100
Current business/daytime tel. no.	0151 789 49141
Health:	Generally excellent – non smoker
Status:	Widower
Holder of clean driving licence	

Hobbies/Interests

Music, theatre, gardening, birdwatching.

Fig. 9. A sample job-specific CV cont.

Updating existing executive CVs

Because of the competition for posts in executive fields, many executives now like to keep their CV up to date, so that even if they are in a job they can take immediate advantage of any promising positions which arise. When you are working in the executive market, it's worth asking your clients whether they wish you to keep a *permanent* copy of their CV on disk, which can be updated regularly. This might well lead to more business, and thus more income, for you.

CHECKLIST

- Check local newspapers to see which day they feature special job market pages, and contact the advertising managers to ask for a rates leaflet.

- Look at your competitors in the local newspapers; see what kinds of names they are using, and devise one for yourself which is memorable and professional sounding.

- Visit the local library, and take out some recently written books on the subject of CV production.

CASE STUDIES

Brian finds a niche

Brian Woods considered himself something of an expert on CVs, given his experience as a departmental manager. He decided to advertise in the 'Professional and Technical' section of his local paper, and also in the 'Situations Vacant' section of the professional magazine to which he subscribes.

There were seven replies to his local newspaper ad, all of which were from people wanting specifically targeted CVs, and two of which were from people targeting the same position. However, only three of those who initially approached him actually asked him to provide CVs, possibly, Brian felt, because he was charging too much.

The advertisement in the accounting magazine yielded only three replies, as well as a letter from the woman running the employment advice service in the magazine, who wanted to talk to Brian about his service with a view to including him in a magazine feature. However, Brian turned down the idea, as he felt that his venture was still in its infancy.

Andrew backs away

Andrew Lloyd thought about the possibility of producing CVs, but decided that he had so little experience of 'real work' that he had no right telling other people how to go about applying for it. He also felt that at 23 he was a little young, and lacked the confidence to deal with the kind of professional people who might want specific CVs.

Alison branches out

Alison's first thoughts on CVs proved to be wide of the mark, because she felt that they could be produced as she was taught to produce them 20 or so years ago. Although she was keen to give the idea a chance, she realised she had to re-learn the process, a thought which filled her with dread as it meant 'unlearning' her old ways. However, after consulting one or two books on the subject, she accepted that, with a little effort, she could arm herself with the necessary expertise.

DISCUSSION POINTS

1. How do you think you might cope with interviewing the wide variety of people with whom CV production might bring you into contact?

2. How much time, effort and money are you prepared to devote to preparing your information pack, bearing in mind that it may well be the deciding factor in whether people choose to use your services?

3. How will you ensure that the information you receive from your clients remains totally confidential? Think about safe storage of tapes and/or notes and Personal Profile forms.

4
Book-Keeping and Accountancy

If you are fortunate enough to be one of those people who didn't just gulp at the title of this chapter and pass hurriedly onto the next – congratulations! You have the means of making a very respectable income, provided either that you are in possession of one of the many good book-keeping programs around, or that you are prepared to invest in one.

Many business people view book-keeping and accounts as almost a foreign langauge. Accounting is probably the least popular of all business practices, so if you are in a position to offer your services to small local companies for just a few hours per week, to cover invoicing, ledger control and banking, you could be worth your weight in gold.

INVESTING IN SOFTWARE

Accounting software comes in all shapes and sizes. You can pay a small fortune for some of the larger programs, or you can pay next to nothing for shareware. If you are unfamiliar with accounting software, I'd suggest you look at some of the better known systems, such as Tas Books or Sage, which will ensure that back-up is there should you need it.

The essential thing to note about accounting software is that it must be capable of letting you run the books for several companies at once. Don't make the mistake of buying a single user program; what you need is a **multi-books** version of your chosen product. Yes, you may pay considerably more for it, but in return, it will be earning for you as soon as you have mastered its complexities. When you look for multi-books systems, make sure you buy a system which allows multi-functions from a single loading. This might sound a little strange, but at least one of the well known systems asks you to load a copy of the program for every set of books you control, which means of course that your hard disk will soon be cluttered up with multiple copies of the same program. Look for a system which allows you to open a new set of accounts files for new customers from within its existing set-up.

A word of caution

Teaching the ins and outs of book-keeping is obviously outside the scope of this book. I am assuming that, as you are reading this chapter, you know about such things. However, if you are one of those adventurous people who has decided to tackle book-keeping because the idea appeals, or because you are generally good with figures, *please* don't make the mistake of assuming that you can buy an accounts package, master it, and then be able to offer a book-keeping service. Accounts packages don't work like that. You need to know the essentials of book-keeping before you attempt to use either a manual or a computerised system. Also, too often, when people take over the financial records of a company, they find that the previous incumbent has left a bit of a muddle, particularly where a company has been without a book-keeping service for some time.

Book-keeping can be quite complex; if you are determined to learn, find an evening class, or arm yourself with a good book on the subject, before you invest in software. Better still, consider studying for the examinations of the Association of Accounting Technicians, which is supported by all the chartered accountancy bodies. There's no point in spending around £100 upwards on a software package only to find that book-keeping isn't for you after all.

FINDING CLIENTS

There are two effective ways of contacting clients for your proposed book-keeping service. Firstly, make use of the 'Business Services' column of your **local newspaper**. If you can afford it, design a display or semi display ad and pay for a series of insertions. Choose those days on which the paper attracts the kind of readership you are aiming at. If it runs a 'Business' section on a particular day, choose that day, and perhaps another day which attracts advertisements from a particular section of the readership. My own local paper has specific days for car sales and agricultural services, in addition to Situations Vacant, and a business section. Think about which business sector you would enjoy working for, and place an ad on that day.

Secondly, make direct contact with potential clients in your area who might be able to use your services. Create some **flyer style leaflets**, printed on coloured paper, which set out details of your service in a punchy, eye-catching way (see Figure 10), and either deliver them in person, or have them distributed (perhaps by insertion into newspapers, courtesy of your local newsagents or to every house on a postal round, courtesy of the local post office). Of course the majority of your flyers will fall on stony ground, so to speak, and be consigned to the nearest bin, but with luck one or two will fall into the hands of the very people you are trying to contact.

BEFUDDLED BY
BOOK KEEPING?

Vexed by VAT?

**Hazel Bennett can help you with
computerised book-keeping
and accounts services
at very realistic prices.
No business too small,
Shambles-sorting a speciality.**

**Call me on
01234 23456
for further details.**

Fig. 10. The kind of punchy flyer which will catch the eye.

KEEPING THE BOOKS

Before you start work for a company, you will need to find out what your duties are likely to be, so that you can be absolutely sure that you are up to it. At its most simple, keeping the books for a small company may involve you in issuing invoices and statements, keeping nominal, sales and purchase ledgers up to date, and sending out payments for goods and services purchased. In addition, you may be responsible for reconciling the bank account, producing trial balances and possibly financial reports and balance sheets. All of these tasks can be easily covered by your accounting software. If the company is registered for VAT, you may also be responsible for administering that (provided of course that you are conversant with the VAT Regulations) and, again, your accounting software will do most of the work for you.

Protecting your files
When working for a number of companies, make judicious use of **passwords** and authority levels, thus ensuring that only you have access to any critical parts of the program. This is to protect you from the result of any deliberate or accidental interventions in the accounts.

Issuing invoices

Invoices are usually issued at the time of supply of goods and services. Most small companies operate on 30 days credit terms, but check before you set up your system for 30 days, particularly if you intend to ask the software to produce **automatic reminders**. Invoices should include the company name and address, details of the goods purchased, and quantity and one-off price, the total price and a note of terms. In addition, if the company is registered for VAT, the invoice *must by law* show the company's VAT registration number. Figure 11 is an example of a simple invoice produced by a computerised accounting package. Very often, such software uses pre-printed forms.

Issuing follow-up statements

Statements are normally issued at the end of the 30 day or other credit period. The idea of statements is to 'remind' customers of what is owed, and to let them know that their credit period has expired. Statements can detail either those invoices which remain unpaid, or all of those incurred during the last credit period, whether paid or unpaid. Your software can be programmed to produce statements automatically, and you should be able to set the defaults to deal with either of the above cases. In addition, your software can be programmed to keep a note of those who persistently fail to pay up on time. It's worth checking with your employer whether or not you will be responsible for chasing up late payments. Cash flow is a major headache for many small businesses. If you feel you can cope with what can, at times, be a somewhat difficult job, it's worth negotiating an additional fee to act as chaser.

Figure 12 reminds Mrs Oneperson that she owes the company a total of £434.75 for recent work, but that her account with the company has

ANYBODY'S BUILDING SERVICES INVOICE
THE HIGH STREET

ANYTOWN	Invoice No.	9601056
Tel 0245 681011	Date of issue	January 31st, 199X
VAT Reg. 01987650		

VAT No. <u>must</u> be included.

Sold to: Invoiced to: (if other than sold to:)
Mrs Mary Oneperson
Somewhere House
Low Street
Anytown

Date of order	Date completed	Terms of payment
27.10.9X	20th January, 199X	30 Days

Date	Details of goods/services	Hours	Per	Total
01.12.9X	To supply and erection of 4ft close board fencing to front of property			
	Material		£245.00	£245.00
	Labour	10	£ 10.00	£100.00
17.12.9X	To repointing and repair of chimney stack using existing bricks	2.5	£ 10.00	£ 25.00

Note: VAT must be separately detailed.

	Sub Total			£370.00
	+ VAT at 17.5%			£64.75
	GRAND TOTAL			£434.75

Thank you for your custom!

Fig. 11. A simple invoice.

ANYBODY'S BUILDING SERVICES
THE HIGH STREET
ANYTOWN   STATEMENT
Tel 0245 681011
VAT Reg. 01987650

Date: 27th February, 199X

Mrs Mary Oneperson
Somewhere House   Period Ending: 29th February, 199X
Low Street
Anytown

Invoice No.	Date	Amount	Status
951211098	01.12.9X	£14.60	Paid
951211099	09.12.9X	£163.90	Paid
9601023	12.01.9X	£900.45	Paid
9601056	31.01.9X	£434.75	Outstanding
		£434.75	**TOTAL OUTSTANDING**

Please remit by return – thank you

Fig. 12. A follow-up statement.
Statements can take a variety of forms. The important thing is that
they include all relevant information.

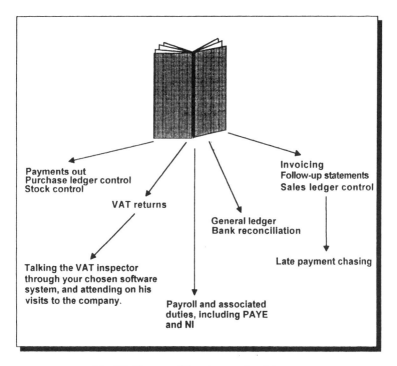

Fig. 13. Your possible roles as a book-keeper.

been worth considerably more. Note that the statement details both invoice numbers and dates, but does not go into detail about the services provided, as that information was included on the original invoice.

QUESTIONS AND ANSWERS

Other advertisements for book-keeping services which I've seen have been rather staid and business-like. Why are you advocating using such a 'punchy' style? Won't this look unprofessional?
The whole point about advertising is that it must be noticed, otherwise there is no point in advertising. For your 'flyer' to work at all, it must attract attention. That's why I advocate coloured paper (so that it doesn't get lost amongst the usual sea of white paper), and that's why I am suggesting eye-catching wording. If, as a qualified accountant, you advertise accountancy services, you'll know that you are bound by a fairly strict code of practice. Book-keepers, however, can afford to be a little more adventurous. Time enough to persuade your potential clients that you are professional when you actually talk to them.

Am I really likely to be held responsible for VAT returns and the like? VAT is a closed book to me at the moment, and I've heard that VAT men are monsters, out to trap the unwary.

To take your last point first, VAT officers are *not* monsters out to trap you. They are merely people doing a job. In my experience, VAT officers are friendly and helpful, and will go to great lengths to advise you, so that you *don't* find yourself on the wrong side of the VAT regulations. The old vision of a crafty VAT officer trying to hoodwink the unwary into committing heaven-knows-what offences was largely fostered by the mischievous tabloid press in the early days of the tax.

As to whether or not you are likely to be held responsible for VAT returns, that is entirely up to you. The people with ultimate responsibility for VAT returns are the company directors, or the company secretary, but should you choose to take over the task, you will be in a position to ask for more money. However, be aware that if you do take on the responsibility for returns, you will also be expected to make yourself available during the visit of the VAT inspector, so that you can answer any questions he may have. For further information, see the section entitled 'Talking to the VAT man'.

You mentioned earlier that people taking over the books of a company often find 'a bit of a muddle'. Is it really up to the newcomer to sort out the mess, and if it is, how should they charge?

On a practical level, all I can say to that is 'If the newcomer doesn't sort out the mess, who will?' I know it doesn't seem fair that you should have to sort out someone else's muddle, but I can't see an alternative. As to charging, there are two schools of thought. The first says that you should charge by the hour for every hour, making the company pay for their apparent lack of care. The second, probably more realistic, is that you should offer to sort things out for a nominal sum, thus engendering the goodwill of the company. I would suggest you make a decision based upon the circumstances at the time. If you feel that the company is trying to take advantage of your good nature, make them pay, but if they are in genuine difficulty, be a bit more lenient.

OFFERING TAX ADVICE

Unless you are a qualified accountant or a tax expert, *don't* be tempted to offer tax advice. The tax position with regard to companies changes constantly, and unless you are involved on a day-to-day basis, you are unlikely to be *au fait* with the current rules and regulations. Similarly, if one of your employers wants advice on his personal tax position, steer well clear of offering any. (That is his responsibility, not yours.) Tax generally is something of a minefield; it is wiser to offer no advice and to preserve your integrity, than to offer incorrect advice and be blamed ever after. If company directors need advice on company or personal taxation, advise them to talk either to their accountant or to an independent financial adviser.

OFFERING PAYROLL SERVICES

Although companies may be computerised as far as word-processing and so forth is concerned, as far as payroll services go, they may well still have a little man with a green eye shade sorting out the salaries! With your accounts/book-keeping skills, you could take over this function. There are specially designed payroll packages around, which calculate all aspects of salaries, including tax and National Insurance. However, if you are skilled in the use of databases, you may well be able to design a package which covers the essentials. Although the set-up cost to the company may seem high, the ongoing charges will be a fraction of what they currently pay a full-time employee. If you'd like to consider this option, take a look at payroll packages to see what they consist of, and whether or not you could design your own, but don't be tempted to offer the service until you are absolutely sure that whichever system you'll employ is capable of doing the job.

TALKING TO THE VAT MAN

'Why', I hear you ask, 'would I want to talk to the VAT man?' Why indeed. Why put the company you work for through all the hassle of VAT registration, and administering the system, if they are below the limit for compulsory registration? The answer is, that by examining a few factors on their behalf, you may be able to save them a considerable amount of money, make their trading base much more sound, and, most importantly, talk yourself into another job. At present, companies are legally obliged to register where their annual turnover exceeds £47,000. However, there are certain classes of business for whom voluntary registration would be useful regardless of turnover.

Voluntary registration

Advantages

● Registered companies give the impression of being far more professional, particularly when dealing with large international companies.

- VAT on capital costs can be reclaimed, even where there is a break between setting up the company and registering for VAT.

- The VAT charged on bought in items can be reclaimed, and can be passed on to the customer in the form of VAT, rather than having to be hidden in the unit charge. This is of particular benefit to companies who regularly buy in either finished goods or components which attract VAT.

Disadvantages

- Administration of VAT requires a considerable amount of work. Returns must be forwarded at regular intervals, and there can be heavy fines for late returns.

- The amount of VAT collected must be considered when looking at the financial situation of the company. Large charged-on items can considerably distort the figures, and cash-flow problems can result from VAT repayment where invoices remain unpaid after the due date, unless you are operating on a 'cash accounting' basis. This can be a particular problem with monthly returns.

- The VAT man will want to visit the company's premises in order to assess the accounting system, to ensure that it is up to standard, and to ensure that VAT is being properly administered. The person responsible for dealing with returns must be present at these visits, which usually occur every two years or so, although there is no hard and fast rule.

H M Customs and Excise produce a series of very useful free pamphlets on the subject of VAT, including one which deals specifically with voluntary registration (700/1/94 *Should I be Registered for VAT?*). It is well worth giving your regional office a ring and asking them for details. Look for them under 'Customs and Excise' in the phone book.

CHECKLIST

- Look for advertisements offering book-keeping services in your area, and telephone one or two of the advertisers to find out the usual scale of charges for such services in your area.

- Take a look at the various accounting software packages on offer. Do they require you to use pre-printed forms, and if so, what is the average cost of these forms?

- Having obtained the various booklets on VAT, look at the whys and wherefores of filing monthly, as opposed to quarterly, returns.

CASE STUDIES

Brian is in his element

Having had some success with producing CVs, Brian decided that he really ought to be using his major subject area to earn what he describes as 'money for old rope'. As a qualified accountant, he was in an excellent position to offer his services as a fully fledged accountant. However, to do so would involve him in applying for a practising certificate, and also in taking out costly professional indemnity insurance – both requirements of his professional body.

By offering extended book-keeping services, Brian was working well within his capabilities, and because he was able to tell his clients during initial interviews that he was qualified, he was able to secure work which others might not have been able to. However, he chose *not* to advertise his credentials because he felt, probably rightly, that potential clients might be put off, fearing prohibitive charges.

Brian took on the task of book-keeper for three local companies, and greatly enjoyed the fact that the work was largely stress-free, because of his expertise and his relatively casual status. Using his considerable spreadsheet knowledge, he was also able to provide them with financial analysis as an adjunct to his other services.

Andrew ducks again

Having rejected the idea of producing CVs, for good reasons, Andrew felt that he ought at least to give the idea of book-keeping some thought. So, he thought. But not for long. 'Anyone trusting me with their books would need their head examining. All I know about double entry book-keeping is that the debits go on the window side. This is definitely not for me.'

Alison tries her hand

Alison's rather tentative foray into CV production has proved to be well worth the effort, and she felt that she was gaining in confidence all the time, and was more and more able to branch out. She had undergone RSA training in book-keeping some years ago, although she had to admit she was a little rusty. After investing in a recently published book on book-keeping, she realised that the job was well within her capabilities.

She decided to spend some of her CV production earnings on an up-to-date Windows accounts package which would enable her to do all of the basic operations. In order to find clients, she produced a batch of leaflets which she fired off to every small company in her area. She also answered an advertisement in the local paper requesting someone to help with book-keeping.

Very soon, Alison found that her approaches were bearing fruit, and she took on the book-keeping for two local companies. After nine months or so, her confidence had grown to such an extent that she persuaded one of the companies to let her extend her duties to managing cash flow and dealing with VAT.

DISCUSSION POINTS

1. Where does book-keeping end and accountancy start? What are the main differences between the two roles?

2. Keeping the books for companies can necessitate the printing out of large documents. Can your printer cope with the necessary tractor-fed paper?

3. If your proposed software package assumes you will make use of pre-printed, multi part forms, it is assuming you have access to a dot matrix printer, so that second and subsequent copies will print out. If this is not the case, how will you get round the problem?

How to Publish a Newsletter
Graham Jones

'Good practical stuff . . . Will certainly give you a good enough understanding of the basics to cope with the normal demands of newsletter publishing.' *Writers News*. 'Until now there has been no adequate British guide . . . but that has been remedied in a new book by Graham Jones, *How to Publish a Newsletter* . . . a comprehensive guide to all aspects including the initial concept, design, writing, marketing, finance, contributors, advertising, editing, printing etc.' *Freelance Writing & Photography*.

£9.99. 176pp illus. 1 85703 166 0. 2nd edition.
Please add postage & packing (UK £1 per copy, Europe £2 per copy, World £3 per copy airmail).
How To Books Ltd, Plymbridge House, Estover Road, Plymouth PL6 7PZ, United Kingdom. Tel: (01752) 202301. Fax: (01752) 202331.
Credit card orders may be faxed or phoned.

5
Getting into Desktop Publishing

LOOKING AT SYSTEM REQUIREMENTS

Getting into desktop publishing can feel a little like getting in with the big boys. Modern DTP software is both disk and memory hungry; to run it successfully, you need a minimum of a 486DX 33MHz machine, with *at least* 200 mb (doubled to 400 mb) of hard disk space and 8 mb of RAM (16 would be even better). This set up will give you the capacity to run your DTP program to its full potential.

Whilst this disk and memory capacity may seem outlandish to those of you running older systems, there are good reasons for it. DTP packages themselves take up lots of disk space and memory because of their powerful nature. In addition, the files they create are enormous. The programs *will* run on less powerful computers, but they'll be excruciatingly slow. If you are going to get into DTP, do it properly. Don't buy a cheap system, then spend the next twelve months regretting it.

CHOOSING YOUR SOFTWARE

You don't have to spend a fortune when buying DTP software, but you do need to look carefully at the features offered by the various programs. DTP is not some magical term, designed to alienate those unfamiliar with aspects of page design. Indeed, if you're using one of the top end word-processing packages, you'll find that DTP offers little which you don't already have. Good DTP packages give you the capacity to manipulate a combination of text, graphics, charts and so on, on your chosen page template or layout. They enable the import and export of a wide variety of text and graphics files from other sources, and offer picture editing, cropping and manipulation. In addition, some offer an infinite variety of bolt-on fonts and graphics, the ability to manipulate text along a variety of curves or circles, and even basic photograph enhancement. Look for all of the above features in a program, and if possible, arrange to view the various programs in action, so that you can make a really informed choice. Don't take the word of the salesman that the package will do what you want. Know what you want before you go shopping, and don't be persuaded to compromise. Your DTP program will, if you choose wisely, open up a whole new world of design potential.

Getting to know your software

With all software, and crucially so with DTP, it is *vital* to spend time getting to know it. Once your system is up and running, spend lots of time exploring, with the software manual next to you. If it's one of the better packages, its capabilities will astound you. If you're anything like me, you'll find yourself working (or should I say playing?) long into the night, constantly discovering new features.

Choosing a printer

If you already own either an **inkjet** or a **laser printer**, skip this section. If not, I have to tell you that a dot matrix printer, whatever the quality, cannot possibly do justice to the output from a DTP package. Beg, borrow, or hire an inkjet printer, and see the difference in output for yourself. I'm not suggesting you buy one right now, but put it on your list of 'things to buy', so that it gets priority when you've started earning.

DEVELOPING AN EYE FOR DESIGN

It could be argued that there is no such thing as 'good design'; that what looks good to one person might look frightful to another. Whilst I agree that there is a subjective element to one's appreciation of design, there are fundamentals which cannot be ignored.

Designing the page

When creating a page design, the first question to ask yourself is 'What kind of people are going to read this?' Think about the age of your target readership. This gives you your first reference point: the font size for the main text. Next, think about the purpose of the publication; is it perhaps a general readership magazine, of local interest only, or is it an academic publication, aimed at a very narrow, well motivated readership? If the latter, straight unadorned text will probably be acceptable, even preferable, but if the former, you'll want to use a variety of headings, to assist your readers to pick out the sections of information relevant to them. The addition of graphics, charts *etc* will all help to give further visual appeal.

In addition to looking good, a page of information should be meaningful and easy to follow. The use of white space on a page makes the page easier to read and assimilate. Take a look at Figure 14.

The Principles of the Computer

The principles behind the modern computer were conceived by Babbage in the 19th century, the first practical machines being built in Britain and America during World War II. Post-war developments in information theory and the invention of the transistor enabled the computer revolution of the next 20 years. Since the 1970s, advances in integrated circuits using silicon chips have led to the development of micro-computers, resulting in price reductions which have enabled computer ownership in a large percentage of the population.

A digital computer processes information in the form of groups of binary numbers which are represented by the on and off positions of electronic switches. The sequence of operations performed on this information is controlled by a program, and the suite of programs that enables a computer to perform useful functions is called its software. The physical equipment, or hardware of a computer generally has three main component parts: the central processor unit or CPU, the main memory, and peripheral devices which enable information to be fed into the machine, display it in a readable form, or act as auxiliary memory.Input, formerly by punched

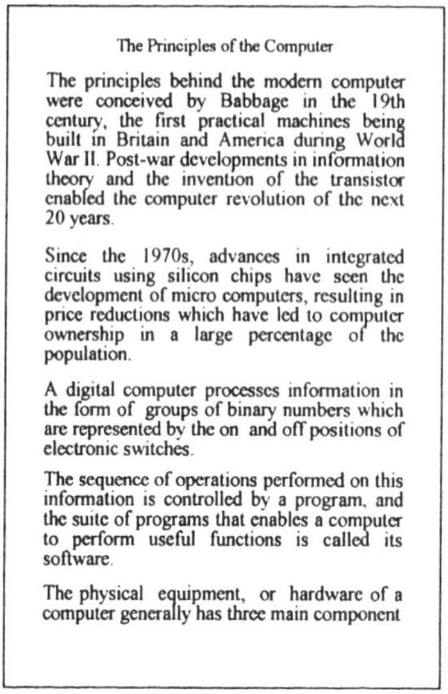

The Principles of the Computer

The principles behind the modern computer were conceived by Babbage in the 19th century, the first practical machines being built in Britain and America during World War II. Post-war developments in information theory and the invention of the transistor enabled the computer revolution of the next 20 years.

Since the 1970s, advances in integrated circuits using silicon chips have seen the development of micro computers, resulting in price reductions which have led to computer ownership in a large percentage of the population.

A digital computer processes information in the form of groups of binary numbers which are represented by the on and off positions of electronic switches.

The sequence of operations performed on this information is controlled by a program, and the suite of programs that enables a computer to perform useful functions is called its software.

The physical equipment, or hardware of a computer generally has three main component

Fig. 14. Page design – the importance of white space.

The information shown on each page is exactly the same, but in the left hand example, it is presented as a page of solid text, with very little surrounding space, and is thus comparatively daunting. In the right hand example, however, the text has been broken up into short paragraphs, with considerable white space dividing each one. As a result, this example is much easier on the eye; the words are not lost in a fog of black and white print.

Spacing the text

All DTP programs offer variable line spacing, or 'leading', which enables the operator to make the best use of text spacing. You'll need to experiment with different fonts to achieve the best effects and readability, but generally, the smaller the font size, the lower the leading. In general terms, the leading should be 20 per cent greater than the point size, although sans serif fonts such as Arial or Helvetica often require more leading to ensure legibility.

Adding graphics and decorative fonts to your page

The use of graphics, pictures, charts *etc* will invariably increase the visual appeal of a page, but not if taken to excess, or used in conjunction with lots of different fonts, 'flashes' and other paraphernalia. Such layouts present your readers with a visual overload of unfathomable information, the net effect being that they are more likely to turn over than to try to grasp the page's meaning. There is a fine line between exciting and over-the-top page design, which beginners often cross in their anxiety to show off their newly acquired potential. One of the easiest ways to liven up a page is to add a logo, or header, using one of your newly acquired decorative fonts. In fact, the temptation to use two or three, or even more, can be overwhelming. Resist it. Nothing gives you away as a beginner more than the overuse of fancy fonts.

What's 'Good' and what's 'Bad'?

Compare Figures 15 and 16. At first glance, the differences appear subtle, but look closely and see if you can spot the answer to the above question. Look at the spacing of the text and graphics for example, and the fonts used. Look at the information on the page. How effective is the second example when compared with the first?

Comparing the pages

The points I'd make are as follows: the graphics in Figure 16 are overlarge, and have the effect of dominating the page rather than enhancing it. This example uses four different fonts, together with large over-fussy font capitals for sentence openers, whereas Figure 15 uses only two fonts: the header font reflecting that used in the sidebar, so that the two tie up on the page. Although the font size used in Figure 16 does act as an eye-catcher, the overlarge text makes the page look unbalanced and top-heavy, particularly in view of the way the important information-giving text lower down the page has been crammed in.

The leading (line spacing) on Figure 15 makes for easy reading, and the eye is led to the next section by the use of bold characters, and white space. That all-important white space is lost in Figure 16.

The real message to be gained from this exercise is 'learn to look'. Use the available space to its best effect, and see your page as a whole, rather than as a series of separate entities. Pick up one or two magazines from the news-stand and see how they go about organising page design. Finally, arm yourself with a good book on DTP (see Further Reading) and study it carefully, paying particular attention to the essentials of good page design.

Once upon a time

... if you were vegetarian, and fancied cheese with your cracker, you could choose Cheddar. Now, thanks to consumer pressure, almost any cheese you can name can be found in supermarket cold cabinets, bearing the label "Suitable for Vegetarians"!

Stilton, the traditional 'after dinner' favourite served with a glass of delicious vintage port, is now sold in most major supermarkets. Blue is more common than white, but keep your eyes open, as white is beginning to appear in more and more cheese cabinets.

Crumbly white Cheshire, creamy Double Gloucester, and even the less commonplace regional cheeses such as Caerphilly, and Wiltshire are now available in selected stores.

If you're seeking something warming and delicious for supper, why not try Rachel MacGregor's delicious **'Parmesan Baked Parsnips'**; wonderful comfort food for a cold winter's evening.

Ingredients:

6 ozs. parsnips, (after peeling) parboiled for 10 minutes
3 free range eggs, size 1 - 2
3 ozs Vegetarian Cheddar cheese
1½ ozs Vegetarian Parmesan Cheese
½ pint creamy milk, *or* ¼ pint single cream with ¼ pint milk
Freshly grated nutmeg to taste
Pinch of dry mustard, + salt and freshly ground pepper to taste

Here's how:

Preheat oven to 350°F or equivalent

Quarter the parsnips, then arrange them over the base of a shallow casserole dish. Sprinkle with nutmeg.
Beat the eggs with the milk and/or cream mixture, then add the Cheddar, and half of the Parmesan
Season to taste with mustard, salt, and pepper, then pour over parsnips
Sprinkle the surface with the remaining parmesan, and bake for 30 - 35 minutes, until golden brown and bubbling.

(sidebar, vertical text:) Anyone for Cheese?

Fig. 15. Good design . . .

Once upon a time

... if you were vegetarian, and fancied cheese with your cracker, you could choose Cheddar. Now, thanks to consumer pressure, almost any cheese you can name can be found in supermarket cold cabinets, bearing the label "Suitable for Vegetarians"!

Stilton, the traditional 'after dinner' favourite served with a glass of delicious vintage port, is now sold in most major supermarkets. Blue is more common than than white, but keep your eyes open, as white is beginning to appear in more and more cheese cabinets.

Wonderfully crumbly white Cheshire, creamy Double Gloucester, and even the less commonplace regional cheeses such as Caerphilly, and Wiltshire are now available in selected stores.

Jf you're seeking something warming and delicious for supper, why not try Rachel MacGregor's delicious **'Parmesan Baked Parsnips'**; wonderful comfort food for a cold winter's evening.

Ingredients:
6 ozs. parsnips, (after peeling) parboiled for 10 minutes
3 free range eggs, size 1 - 2
3 ozs Vegetarian Cheddar cheese
$1^1/_2$ ozs Vegetarian Parmesan Cheese
$^1/_2$ pint creamy milk, *or* $^1/_4$ pint single cream with $^1/_4$ pint milk
Freshly grated nutmeg to taste
Pinch of mustard, + salt and freshly ground black pepper to taste.

Here's how:
Preheat oven to 350°F
Quarter the parsnips, then arrange them over the base of a shallow casserole dish. Sprinkle with nutmeg.
Beat the eggs with the milk and/or cream mixture, then add the Cheddar and half of the Parmesan
Season to taste with mustard, salt and pepper, then pour over parsnips
Sprinkle the surface with the remaining parmesan, and bake for 30 - 35 minutes, until golden brown and bubbling.

Fig. 16. . . . and bad.

APPROACHING POTENTIAL CLIENTS

I would suggest that the most profitable way of obtaining DTP work is to approach organisations and businesses *direct*, sending them examples of your work. Think carefully about those examples, and make them work for you. When thinking about word processing, we looked at brochures, newsletters *etc* but with your added scope, you can offer so much more.

Producing samples

Look around you, and see how many local organisations make use of a readily identifiable **logo**. Look at those which don't, and design some eye-catching ideas for them, using your software's drawing and text manipulation tools to their full capacity. Produce some eye-catching advertising **posters**, featuring your newly-designed logos, and send them off to the general manager of the organisation in question. Don't just address your package to 'The General Manager'. Find out the name of this person by telephoning the organisation. Follow up this approach with a phone call a few days later and, if the manager liked your ideas, see if he'll agree to a meeting to discuss the future production of stationery and advertising material.

Showing your worth

Another effective way of obtaining work is to approach potential clients when they are in the exact situation where you might be able to help them out next time. For instance, if you find yourself at an antiques fair, take a look at the hand-outs. Can you do better? Take two or three of the not-so-good ones home with you. Work hard at producing really effective replacements, then send them to the potential client with a covering letter telling them that this is how *you* would have produced their leaflets. Follow that up with the suggestion that you will do their next lot for them at a reduced fee. If they're happy (how could they fail to be?) the job will be yours. Make sure that your name appears on the leaflets (and in fact on *everything* you produce) and with luck, others will contact you, with offers of further work.

Wasting time?

You might argue that the production of sample packs for organisations is a dreadful waste of valuable time. After all, you could be earning. However, the more time you spend practising your skills in this area, the more expert you are likely to become, and the quicker you'll be able to produce the goods. Don't resent the time spent in producing samples, it really is worth while both from the point of view of the work it may bring in and in terms of your increasing expertise.

DESIGNING THE PACKAGE

One of the first DTP jobs I did was for a local charity. I produced matching posters, leaflets and tickets for a Christmas concert. I also produced carol sheets which used some of the art work on the posters, but had elements of their own in addition. This combined approach was extremely effective; the posters were produced on bright yellow A3 card, so that no one could claim not to have seen them, and the other elements were produced on a soft blue 100 gsm paper. The job didn't pay particularly well, but the whole thing took me less than an hour to produce, excluding printing, and brought me in a considerable amount of other, better paid work as a direct result.

Whenever you produce dummies of any sort, think about how you might be able to produce a combination of products in order to maximise your impact. If you decide to approach shops, produce promotional leaflets combined with money-off coupons for instance. Newsletters might be combined with hand-outs; letter heads with compliment slips. Whichever route you choose, for maximum impact think about a combined approach. It is *always* much more effective.

QUESTIONS AND ANSWERS

You talk about 'white space' on the page. Surely including lots of white space means that you use much more paper. And what happens where you are given a maximum number of pages, and no flexibility of the text? Yes, you're right, white space does mean more paper, but you shouldn't look upon that as meaning *wasted* paper. Conversely, I'd argue that, without judicial use of white space, what you'll waste will be your time and effort, because people simply won't bother to read what you've written. With regard to your second point: where space is at a premium, reduce the leading, and if necessary the margin and paragraph spacing. Or another way to minimise the space the words themselves take up is to alter the text tightness. This is a mechanism employed by DTP programs which allows you to alter the amount of space between letters and words. The settings offered vary, but are generally 'tight', 'normal' or 'loose'. A 'tight' text setting, which is approximately 90 per cent of 'normal' spacing, can save you perhaps two lines in every twelve, and will be imperceptible to the average reader. Look at your particular program to see how this works.

The Fish Plaice
Price List

Plaice	£0.00
Large Cod	£0.00
Small cod	£0.00
Haddock	£0.00
Large fries	£0.00
Standard fries	£0.00
Salmon fish cakes	£0.00
Mushy Peas	£0.00

The Fish Plaice
November Special
FREE STANDARD FRIES
WITH EVERY LARGE COD
Make this the month you meet us!

The Fish Plaice
34 Dock Street, Ipswich
Tel. 01473 778778

Open Monday to Saturday
11.30 am - 1.30 pm
5.00 pm - 11.30 p.m.

The Fish Plaice could make a splash with some imaginatively designed co-ordinating flyers.

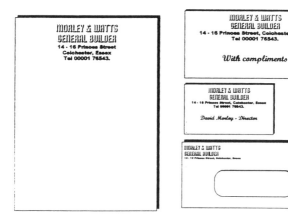

Messrs. Morley & Watts, out to create a good impression with co-ordinated stationery.

Fig. 17. Two examples of a co-ordinated approach. No graphics are included in the examples, but there is no reason why you should not use them, as long as they fit into the overall theme.

A colour printer is beyond my means at the moment, but I'm sure that companies looking for effective advertising will insist upon colour. How do I cope with this?

If you had a colour printer and were to use it for advertising posters and so forth, you might well price yourself out of the market, as colour printing is still much more expensive than black and white. The way to optimise black and white print is to use large bold text on coloured paper. For advertising purposes, the brighter the better. For other purposes, use coloured paper whenever possible, to differentiate your output from that of others. If you do lots of work for one organisation, use different shades of the same colour, which will act as a subconscious 'flag' in people's memories.

Can you tell me about 'house style'. What is it exactly, and how do I learn it?

The term 'house style' simply means a set of fixed rules adopted by a 'house' or organisation. For instance, they may always use one colour stationery, blue text, a particular font, and have fixed rules of grammar to which all must adhere. When you accept work, particularly for larger organisations, you should ask about their existing house style. If they look blank, try to develop a style which you'll use for all their work. The idea of 'house style' is that it makes all output look similar, and thus cohesive and businesslike. Again, it can act as a subconscious 'flag', so that readers will know immediately that a leaflet or whatever comes from a certain company.

CHECKLIST

- Create a dummy page with your DTP software, incorporating as many features as you can find. Include such features as charts, drawings, layered frames, manipulated text *etc*. Don't worry too much about page design at this stage, just practise using the various features your package offers.

- Look at the example featuring The Fish Plaice. Design a 'Special Offer' poster for them, making full use of the graphics potential your package offers.

- Print out your design on various qualities of paper. Print it out onto coloured paper or card. See which creates the most immediate impression, and why.

CASE STUDIES

Brian broadens his horizons

Brian had never met DTP, and was a little afraid of the idea until he vis-
ited a local newspaper office and was able to see at first hand how they
produced their weekly issues. He decided to buy the cheapest package
he could find which would do the job, and was surprised to discover that
it cost him well under £100.00. It didn't have all the features offered by
larger, more expensive packages, but Brian felt that many of these features would remain unused even if he did have access to them.

His first foray into finding work was to talk to friends in the village,
one of whom owned a tropical fish centre, and the other a pet shop. Both
expressed an interest as long as the price was reasonable, *ie* low, because
as both said, 'We are just beginning to come out of recession, and we
don't want to jeopardise our financial position'. Brian was able to design
distinctive packages for both people.

The pet shop owner had been looking for someone to produce gift
vouchers redeemable only in her shop, and Brian designed and produced
vouchers which were then stamped with a rolling number stamper, using
red ink, to prevent forgery.

The tropical fish centre owner asked Brian to produce a range of literature, including a 24-page A5 brochure, detailing care and feeding of
the various fish. Brian found this much more of a challenge, but perse-
vered, and found the job rewarding, both in terms of the amount he
learned, and the amount he earned.

Andrew – happy at last

Having studiously avoided both CV and book-keeping work, Andrew
welcomed the idea of going into DTP with open arms as it gave him the
scope to use his design skills to the full. Rather than approach run-of-
the-mill organisations with 'safe' projects, he decided to design posters
and flyers for a small independent theatre company which was visiting
his home town. He designed on spec and approached them during their
run, his aim being that his advertising material could be circulated to
various small theatres in the country, in order to publicise the group. The
members of the company expressed themselves delighted with his
efforts, and agreed to a trial run of 100 posters. Although the job wasn't
as lucrative as Andrew had hoped, he could see that there was plenty of
potential in what was a largely untapped area.

Alison plays safe – and makes a profit

Having been very successful in word-processing, Alison decided to
advertise for DTP work amongst existing clients. She designed leaflets

which she mailed to all existing clients, and also included in any completed work she sent out.

Because her work was known and trusted, she found she was approached by several organisations anxious to make use of her talents. Her previous DTP work stood her in good stead, and because she was practised, she found even the more exacting jobs were completed in a relatively short time. Her earnings rose steadily, and she was able to buy a much coveted colour printer, which would enable her to follow up one of her own ideas.

DISCUSSION POINTS

1. How do others in your locality offering DTP charge for their services? If they charge by the hour, do you think this would be appropriate for you as a beginner? What, if any, are the alternatives?

2. In what way does the use of alternative fonts effect the overall look and feel of a document?

3. Would you be prepared to work on a voluntary basis, say for a charity, if it gave you the opportunity to develop your skills?

6
Making Use of Photocopiers

THINKING ABOUT PHOTOCOPIERS

When you start taking in work, particularly DTP work, you may well find that you need access to high quality photocopying facilities with increasing regularity. If you live close to those facilities, perhaps a local copyshop or the local library for instance, this may not be a problem. However, for many of us, such facilities are not easily available, and we must therefore consider owning our own machine.

There are two kinds of commonly used machine: the larger 'office' models, which enlarge and reduce, and have the facility to offer a limited form of colour reproduction using a process known as 'masking', or the smaller 'home office' or 'personal' models, which do not generally enlarge or reduce.

OBTAINING THE BEST FOR LESS

When buying a photocopier, you should get the best you can afford. The larger **office machines** will give you much better facilities than the smaller machines, but they are prohibitively expensive to buy. However, there are ways round the expense. With so many companies going out of business at the moment, office copiers can be picked up fairly cheaply, if you know where to look.

Where to go

There are three main sources of information and supply. Firstly, keep an ear to the ground, and an eye on the local newspaper columns, which often carry public information notices about companies going out of business. When you spot a likely candidate, don't hesitate. Phone the office, and ask whether they have a photocopier for sale. Very often, when firms go into receivership, their assets will end up at auction, being sold for next to nothing. However, if you can get in before that happens and offer a reasonable price, it may be that the photocopier will be yours instead of disappearing into a black hole, to re-emerge later at a considerably inflated price, having been bought by one of the many dealers who buy up such goods at auction.

Buying at auction

Secondly, keep an eye on the local paper for 'computer auctions'. These occur at various sites across the country, and are usually held once a month. Although they call themselves 'computer auctions', they tend to include many items which fall into the category of office equipment. Catalogues are normally available, at minimal cost, before the date of the sale, so that potential buyers can find out what is being offered.

Where auction houses are selling items from a company which has gone out of business, the goods are often sold at ridiculously knock-down prices, so you should be able to find yourself a bargain. However, if you do buy at auction, make *absolutely sure* that the photocopier you hope to buy actually works, as many auctions offer no redress in the event of non-working equipment being bought. This really is a case of 'let the buyer beware'.

Buying via the second hand columns

Most local newspapers carry an 'Office Equipment' section in their classified ads. The drawback of buying from such ads is that the price is likely to be steep. Most of these advertisements come from people who deal in photocopiers to make a living, rather than from one-off sellers, who might simply want to exchange machines. If you decide to answer an ad, don't be tempted to spend more than you can afford, and make absolutely sure that any photocopier offered is really up to the job you require it to do. Don't be afraid to ask questions, and ask for a demonstration, so that you can check copy quality and ease of use. Above all, ask for a written service warranty of some sort, so that should the copier not be up to standard you have some redress.

With regard to copy quality – when you look at a photocopier's output, check that black really means black, not dark grey, when the copier is correctly adjusted. There are various technical reasons why copiers produce grey, all of them bad news in an older copier. If you are offered such a copier, refuse it.

Servicing your machine

However you obtain your second hand office copier, arrange for regular servicing without delay. If you're lucky, the existing service engineer will carry over his services of the machine. If not, talk to the person at your nearest copy shop. In many cases, the copy shop owner does servicing as a sideline, but if he doesn't, he is sure to know of someone who can help. Don't fail to do this, thinking that you won't encounter problems. Photocopiers can be tricky, and they have a nasty habit of letting you down when you need them most. Servicing costs money of course, but remember, your photocopier will be earning for you. As long as you do your sums, the photocopier and its upkeep will pay for themselves, but you *must* keep the machine maintained, as copy quality deteriorates at an alarming rate if the machine is not looked after.

Looking at simpler machines

If you simply cannot contemplate buying an office machine, or do not have the room to store such a bulky item, think about one of the smaller **home office** machines produced by copier manufacturers. These machines cost in the region of £300-£500, so they are not a minor purchase, but for the most part they are entirely trouble free, and the copy quality is excellent. Their obvious drawback however is that they are straight copiers only, so if you wanted to enlarge or reduce, you would have to use a machine at a copy shop or printers. Look for the kind which offers multiple copying, as many of the cheaper ones will copy only one sheet at a time, and are thus time consuming if you want several copies of the same original.

. . . and their benefits

One of the main benefits of these smaller machines is that they have **toner cartridges** which incorporate the copier mechanism, which means that when the cartridge is replaced, after 3000 or so copies, the photosensitive drum, the development unit and the cleaning unit are also replaced. This means that copy quality remains excellent for the life of the machine. (Many office copiers produce poor quality copies after just a few years service, as their components become worn, and replacement of the components can be very expensive.)

Required maintenance of these machines is virtually non-existent, but the supplier is usually able to offer advice about servicing, should it be required. Conversely, talk to the man at your nearest copy shop.

Large versus small – pros and cons

Let's sum up the advantages of owning a large office copier, rather than a small personal one.

Advantages

● The machine is much more versatile, and will enable you to enlarge and reduce.

- You can copy a wider variety of sizes of paper.

- The machine will cope with much larger quantities – useful for volume work.

- Sorting can be automated.

- The machine can be hired out specifically for copying, thus earning income.

Disadvantages

- It could cost three to four times the price of a personal copier.

- It would take up a great deal of space, and would need a large solid table or cabinet to house it.

- Machine components wear with time, and are expensive to replace.

- Machine requires regular servicing to maintain copy quality.

- Once people realise you have a copier, you tend to be targeted by those needing copying.

HIRING MACHINES FOR ONE-OFF TASKS

I cannot emphasise enough the importance of making contact with, and preferably friends with, your local copy shop owner or printer. When you are offered a job which requires the use of a process to which you do not have access, you can take the job as long as you know that the work can be done locally.

Hiring machines for one-off tasks can be more expensive, particularly if you are thinking of colour copies, but your client will be paying, not you. One of the tasks for which reducers might be used, for instance, is the reduction of an A4 image down to A5 size. This is of particular value where good graphics resolution is required, as the reduction process considerably improves resolution. Another reduction task might be the reduction of A3 computer printouts to more manageable A4 size.

Producing enlargements
If you are producing advertising posters, you may well decide to produce them as A3 or larger, in order to increase both their visibility and

impact. Use the best grade of card or paper the machine will accept, as large sheets are much more prone to tearing because of their unwieldly nature. Stick to coloured stock where you can.

QUESTIONS AND ANSWERS

You haven't mentioned paper. Don't photocopiers require the use of special, expensive, paper?
No, they don't. The paper sold as copier paper is generally cheap, light-ish in weight, and offered in a variety of colours. However, most modern copiers will copy onto any paper, up to a given weight for the machine. My only reservation would be – don't attempt to copy onto finest grade wove papers, as the copy image is likely to rub off because of the uneven surface of the paper.

You mentioned 'masking' as a method of colour copying. What does this entail?
'Masking' is a method by which copy can be produced in a variety of colours, usually a maximum of four. It is a time consuming process, which involves the production of four original sheets, each of which will have various areas blanked off so that they don't print. For example, suppose you want to print a blue bottle with a yellow label, the first original would show only the blue bottle, with the label area masked. The second would show only the label area, with the bottle masked. In order to produce the required colour copy, the ink colour would have to be changed after each colour was printed onto the copy. As I said, time consuming, and very fiddly.

I live quite close to a good copy shop, and find it generally convenient to visit. Why should I buy a copier?
Simple, you shouldn't unless you find the cost of using the copy shop prohibitive (although if you are costing out your work so that the client pays each time, I can't see a problem). The only argument for owning your own copier in these circumstances is the convenience of having it there. As long as you're organised, and take a whole batch to the copy shop rather than making three or four trips for one sheet at a time, I would continue as you are doing.

What about the new colour copiers? Should I think about buying one of those?
Yes, if you have several thousand pounds to spare; otherwise, forget it. The copies they give are stunningly good, but very expensive. One-offs

at a shop near me cost nearly £1.00 each. The machines themselves cost over £10,000, so you can see why owners have to charge such high rates. It might be worth thinking about a second hand machine, but they really haven't been around long enough to bring the price down to a sensible level. The only thing I would say in favour of buying a colour copier is that you might be able to recoup your initial costs by hiring out the machine. However, it would take a *very* long time to recover £10,000 unless you had your own copy shop or printshop. Frankly, I should forget the whole idea, it's just not cost effective.

CHECKLIST

● Take a look at the copying facilities in your area, and weigh up the various prices. Is one shop consistently cheaper for their whole range of services, or would you need to shop around to get the best deal for the size or volume you wanted to copy?

● Look at your office set-up, and think about where you might house a copier. Remember that personal copiers take up much less room than office copiers. Think also about paper storage. The paper needs to be stored in a warm dry place in order to maintain copy quality. Do you have the facilities, or could you arrange them?

● Even if you cannot contemplate buying a copier at the moment, get into the habit of checking the second hand columns for copiers, so that you can gauge the prices being asked.

CASE STUDIES

Brian's conscience troubles him, but not enough

Brian Woods was fortunate in that he was able to use the photocopiers at the office of his previous employer, as he still worked for them occasionally on a consultancy basis. The copiers offered far more facilities than personal copiers, and although at times he felt like something of a free-loader, he wasn't so troubled that he'd give up the facility.

Andrew's conscience doesn't

Andrew also had access to a large office photocopier, but in his case, at his old college. As an ex-student, Andrew was able to use the copier at a favourable rate, and although it meant a ten mile round trip, he felt it was more sensible than buying his own copier, as long as he took his copies in batches. Where he desperately needed extra copies of output, he printed them out on his printer, rather than take the trip into town.

Alison thanks her lucky stars

Some time ago, when Alison started working for a local charity, she advertised in the newspaper for a copier, hoping to get one for a knock-down price. To her great delight, she was offered a free, though some-what elderly, machine. After paying to have it renovated, she found it fulfilled all her needs, although the need for continuous maintenance of what was, after all, an old machine could sometimes be a headache.

DISCUSSION POINTS

1. Is it cheaper to produce multiple copies from a photocopier, or from your printer? Take a look at the relevant costs.

2. 'You don't need a photocopier. It's just as easy to produce multiple copies of documents using your computer printer'. Is this statement as true as it first appears?

3. If you own an office type copier, it's very tempting to think that you might advertise its use, in order to recoup some of the expense of the purchase. What might be the disadvantages of such a move?

7
Using Databases

EXPLAINING THE DATABASE

A database is, well, a base or storage system for data. It's that simple. Or to put it another way, a database is an organised collection of information. The information can be virtually anything, from names, addresses, illnesses, fruits, makes of car, engine sizes, anything at all you care to think of. The term 'relational' used in conjunction with database means that links between one area of a database and another can be established so that any information put into one area is automatically updated or reflected in the other. In this chapter, we are going to look at the uses to which 'relational', rather than the less sophisticated 'flat-file' databases, can be put.

Examining its uses

A database can be used to structure name and address lists, client lists, stock lists, transaction lists, lists of collections, lists of goods and their values, as I said, almost anything you care to name. So, companies might welcome the opportunity to have a computerised record of all their clients, for instance, coupled with a linked record of all their transactions. Local nurseries might welcome a stock list incorporating buying, pruning and care tables. Record or book shops might welcome the idea of being able to keep track of their permanent stock, with the option of adding new and deleting old. This is what databases are all about, the making and keeping of efficient records.

CREATING CLIENT LISTS

Suppose you were asked by Davidson Hawes Limited, a local company, to create a client list which would be easily updateable in the future, either by you or by a designated member of their permanent staff. How would you go about it?

The principle behind the creation of databases is that you decide what form the input information will take, then you create 'fields' for the various sectors of information. Let's look at an example (see Figure 18).

Field no.	Field name	Field size	Field type
1	Customer no.	12	Alphanumeric
2	Surname	30	Alphanumeric
3	First name	15	Alphanumeric
4	Other initials	10	Alphanumeric
5	House name/no.	20	Alphanumeric
6	Road name	25	Alphanumeric
7	District	15	Alphanumeric
8	Town	15	Alphanumeric
9	County	15	Alphanumeric
10	Postcode	10	Alphanumeric
11	Tel no.	12	Alphanumeric
12	Last purchase	*	Numeric/currency
13	Purchase value	*	Numeric/currency
14	Credit record	50	Alphanumeric
15	Future action	50	Alphanumeric

Fig. 18. An example of field types and widths. An alphanumeric field is one in which either letters or numbers can be inserted. Such fields cannot be used to create numerical links in the database, so cannot be used to produce calculations based upon input information.

Although the database set up will ask you how many characters, *ie* numbers and/or letters you want to allocate to each field, the field widths can be varied once the database is up and running, so the initial width of the field isn't crucial. However, it's easier to set it up correctly from the first, rather than having to keep going back to increase the field width because you've miscalculated how much space you might need. (Also note that the database does not allow you to choose a field width where you are inputting numeric values, as it creates the width according to the number of characters input.) Now, having decided what our example database should contain in the way of information, let's look at how that information might translate onto a database page (see Figure 19).

On the database page itself, the inner boxes would be the 'active' boxes, into which the relevant information would be placed. The person doing the client list input would record all the relevant details of the first person on the list onto page 1 of this particular file, then go to a new page for each new client.

Let's suppose that Mr Hawes has now looked at the database created for him, and has expressed himself quite pleased, but with reservations. How might we improve this database for him? What we could do is to link 'Last purchase' with 'Total purchase', so that each time his client buys another product or peripheral, that total purchases box is automatically updated. We could also provide a link for *all* 'total purchases' boxes, which would enable us to produce a record of the entire purchases for any given period. These are two very simple examples of links in a relational database.

Sorting the information

In addition to presenting the information on the page in a useful and readable form, any good database will allow you to *sort* information in any order. So, although Mr Hawes wants the information sorted by 'Surname' for his report, it is more use to Mr Davidson if it is sorted by 'County', so that he can assess which counties across the country are producing the most business. If Mr Davidson then decides that he'd like each county broken down into individual sales reps' areas, it would be a simple task to create a field for the rep's name and to input that information into each record. Mr Davidson could then have his wish, as the database could be sorted first by 'Sales Rep' and then by county, or purchase value, or by whatever else took his fancy.

Expanding on the information

Mr Davidson is a rather demanding chap. Having extracted the information he required regarding individual sales reps, he now wants a breakdown of all purchases, so that he can sort out which products are selling and which are not. The way this information could be organised is by linking a separate hidden database behind the original client list, which would be accessed by either a previously programmed hot key or an active button programmed into the database page. This hidden database could quite easily be programmed to produce the required information, and if Mr Davidson wanted it to be for his eyes only, it could include a password to which only he had access.

What the above information tells us is that modern database packages are very powerful tools in the right hands, and there is little which is beyond their scope.

CREATING STOCK LISTS

Both Mr Hawes and Mr Davidson are delighted with the results of your

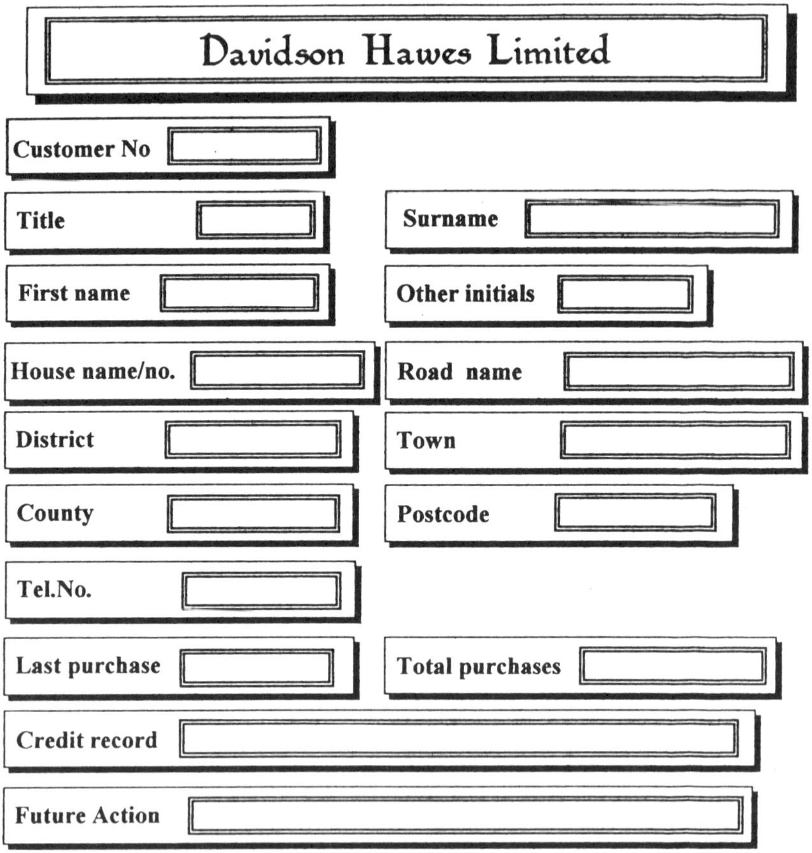

Davidson Hawes Limited

Customer No [ ]

Title [ ]   **Surname** [ ]

First name [ ]   **Other initials** [ ]

House name/no. [ ]   **Road name** [ ]

District [ ]   **Town** [ ]

County [ ]   **Postcode** [ ]

Tel.No. [ ]

Last purchase [ ]   **Total purchases** [ ]

Credit record [ ]

Future Action [ ]

Fig. 19. A typical database page.

efforts so far, but Mr Hawes is a bit miffed because, although Mr Davidson can keep detailed records of purchases, *he* has no way of controlling records of stock. Let's look at how we might create a rolling stock list for him, which will include both incoming and outgoing goods, stock values, and an order prompt, for when stocks of bought-in components are beginning to run down. The kind of information we'd need to include is shown in Figure 20.

Field no.	Field name	Field size	Field type
1	Component name	30	Alphanumeric
2	Current stock level	*	Numeric
3	Normal stock level	*	Numeric
4	Supplier	20	Alphanumeric
5	Goods out – quantity	*	Numeric
6	Goods out – date	12	Alphanumeric
7	Goods in – quantity	*	Numeric
8	Goods in – date	12	Alphanumeric
9	Component net value	*	Numeric/currency
10	Stock net value	*	Numeric/currency
11	Order prompt quantity	12	Alphanumeric

Linked fields, to automate prompting (labelling fields 2 and 3)

Fig. 20. The information fields for the control of stock.

Using those fields, we ought to be able to create a database which will fulfil all Mr Hawes' criteria. Field 12 would be linked with field 3, and would create an automatic order prompt when a programmed minimum quantity was reached. Any of the numeric fields could be linked with any other numeric fields to provide running totals of required information, either of stock numbers, or values. Note that the 'Order prompt quantity' field is alphanumeric rather than numeric, which means that it cannot accidentally be included in any calculations.

DESIGNING SPECIFIC DATABASES

We've looked at two fairly simple examples of the uses to which database programs can be put. Once you become really experienced in using the software, the possibilities are virtually endless. For the expert user, the addition of a 'runtime' version of the program in question will enable you to create 'free-standing' programs which others might run to keep track of almost anything you care to name. (Different software producers have different names for this 'bolt on' to the original program, which is aimed at advanced users, or programmers, but in all cases, it allows the production of free-standing versions of the software.) A free-standing program is one which the potential user could load into his or her own computer, and use without needing to run the whole database program upon which it was designed. If you moved into this market, you could make a great deal of money, particularly if you decided that your program was worth marketing, rather than simply being used by one or two individuals.

Who needs it?
With a 'runtime' version, you might create database programs for a huge variety of hobbyists, any group of which might request very specific functions. To give just one example: bird watchers might welcome a database listing every type of resident, visitor, rare visitor, and a few more besides, into which they could record their sightings. Twitchers are a dedicated lot, and if you were able to combine the basic information with a full description, sighting records, and possibly a picture of the bird, you would appeal to a very wide audience. (However, incorporating even 'thumbnail' pictures into databases makes them very system hungry.)

QUESTIONS AND ANSWERS

What are 'flat file' databases, and how do they differ from relational databases?
A 'flat-file' database is one which allows the production of lists, and offers the same facilities for sorting the information, but does not have the potential for linkage of one field to another. 'Flat-file' database software is usually much cheaper than relational, but is of considerably less value in terms of its potential as a organisation tool.

Newer Windows versions of databases seem to me to be much more complex than the old style Dos programs. Are they really of greater benefit?
My own feeling is that any Windows program is better than its Dos equivalent because, to some extent at least, it is intuitive to learn and use. The real benefit of Windows databases is that much of the programming work required to set up either links within individual databases, or a series of linked databases, is already done for you, whereas with Dos programs the programming had to be done by the user. That means that the program can be developed into a major power tool much more readily.

If I were to set up databases for companies to use, wouldn't those companies have to have access to the database program before they could update the information?
If the company in question wanted you to update the information for them, with information supplied periodically by them, then no, they wouldn't need their own copy of the program. However, if they wanted a designated user of their own to update, they *would* need a copy, and where several people were using the program via a local network, they would need one copy, plus a network licence, allowing a given number of people to access the program.

PRODUCING STATIC DATABASES

A static database is a database which, once set up and supplied with information, remains largely unaltered, other than being updated once or twice a year perhaps. Examples might be the contents of a library, an art gallery, a museum or even a zoo. The list might detail source, insured value, current value or indeed almost anything. Such records prove themselves time and time again in the event of burglary or fire. However, one note of caution: access to such records would need to be very carefully monitored, via the use of security codes or passwords, as unauthorised access would give 'Burglar Bill' invaluable information about which places he might profitably visit.

TEACHING DATABASE USERS

When you find yourself in the happy position of having designed the required database for your client, you may find that he wishes you to keep it up to date by inputting new information periodically, or he may ask you to teach others in his organisation to use the software. Teaching individuals or small groups is relatively simple, and extremely rewarding, but be wary about agreeing to teach large groups if you are not used to such tasks. Group dynamics always seem to dictate that someone in the group is determined to be awkward, or to make a name for themselves. Unless you know how to handle such situations, insist upon one-to-one or small group teaching.

Charging for teaching
Your charges for teaching should reflect your expertise; do not undervalue yourself by charging less than the going rate. You're in business to make money, remember, just as your clients are. Rates for teaching vary enormously: at the time of writing, a lecturer friend charges £10.00

– £15.00 an hour for extra curricular teaching, which he considers low. Another friend charges up to £50.00 per hour, depending upon the complexity of the teaching and the size of the organisation. Obviously, without professional status you'd have difficulty charging the latter, but you could make quite a respectable income by charging the former.

CHECKLIST

● Like other software packages, databases vary considerably, both in price and in performance. Assess those currently available, and see which would provide you with the tools to create the kind of databases we've talked about.

● Think about applications to which you might put a database program in your own home or business, then consider how those applications might be augmented to make them appeal to local organisations.

● The most beneficial way of attracting clients to the possibilities offered by databases is by presenting them with relevant proposals. Select one or two local organisations of disparate nature, and produce dummy applications for them.

CASE STUDIES

Brian produces the goods

Having produced such excellent work for the tropical fish centre, Brian was moved to ask about the possibility of producing a database of stock fish, suppliers' names and addresses, value, feeding and care, and stock levels. The fish centre owner was delighted, declaring that such information would be invaluable to him. However, being a suspicious Norfolk man, he hummed and ha'd about the cost. He and Brian came to an agreement: Brian would work for two hours each evening until the database was finished. He'd work more or less at his own pace, rather than at a pace demanded by his client, and would charge only a nominal rate per hour.

The whole job took Brian almost three weeks to complete, and he presented his client with a variety of listings, and a bill for £100.00, which represented around £3.50 per hour. Although the rate was rather low, Brian saw the job as a learning experience. Whilst compiling the database he was able to explore the software in order to link various aspects of the listings, and to incorporate a hidden database, which covered stock levels and values. He also enjoyed the fact that he learned a great deal about his subject matter.

Andrew finds his enthusiasm dampened

Although Andrew had never used databases, he was very impressed with their potential. Before making any decisions about whether to purchase a package, he decided to test the potential market.

Because it was a special interest area of his, he contacted two classic car showrooms in his area. He suggested to them that they might like access to a database detailing the whereabouts of known classic cars above a certain value, coupled with a list of contacts in the business, so that they had immediate access to information about available cars should collectors need it. Unfortunately for Andrew, however, both showrooms were linked to a national database detailing just the kind of information he proposed. His mistake had been to contact franchised organisations which would already have organised their computer needs. Needless to say, he was very disappointed, but accepted that he'd been driven by his own enthusiasm about classic cars, rather than by practical considerations.

Alison says 'No'

'Look, what's the point of me buying more software, to take on more work, when I'm doing very nicely thank you, with what I'm doing? When I feel the need for a change of direction, I might look at database work as the next step, but until them I'll stick with what I know. The real point is that changing direction means a temporary lull in income, so it needs careful planning.'

DISCUSSION POINTS

1. Thinking about Alison's point – that a change of direction means 'a temporary lull in income' – how might you overcome the problem of trying to learn a new package, whilst continuing with existing work?

2. How would you go about producing a database capable of providing Brian's tropical fish centre client with all the information he requires? Think about the necessary fields, and the possible links within the database, and also the methods of sorting the information which might prove useful to him.

3. Although on this occasion poor old Andrew's efforts proved fruitless, he is generally right in aiming his services at more unusual

outlets. Think about such outlets which might be accessible to you. What kind of area do you live in? Is there something inherent in the locality which you might use to your advantage? For instance, if you live in an agricultural area, how might local farms use your database services?

SPECIAL NOTE

When you become involved in the production of client or other lists which include names and addresses, or other personal information about people, you must register with the **Data Protection Registrar**. Failure to do so could result in heavy fines. Write to them at:

Data Protection Registrar
Springfield House
Water Lane
Wilmslow
Cheshire SK9 5AX.
Tel: (01625) 535777.

8
Making the Most of Labelling Programs

LOOKING AT THE SOFTWARE

'Oh no!', I hear you cry, 'not more software to buy'. Well, I'm pleased to tell you that you don't have to buy labelling programs to produce really imaginative and useful labels of all varieties. However, you do need either to own one of the word processing packages which incorporates Avery label templates or one for which Avery are able to supply a formatting guide (see Appendix) or to be able to format your word-processing page so that it exactly resembles a page or strip of the kind of labels you want to print.

If none of the above applies to you, don't despair. Labelling programs have dropped quite dramatically in price since they were introduced some three or four years ago, with the Windows version of the most popular, Avery LabelPro®, now widely available for little more than £20.00. Given its capabilities, which include graphics, bar coding, sequential numbering and the importation of address and other lists, it is well worth considering if you plan to break into the labelling market.

CREATING LABELS ON BLANK PAGES

Formatting a page for the creation of a certain size of label might strike you as difficult, but it's relatively simple as long as you know your way around the creation and management of frames in your word processor package.

Here's how:

1. Look at the sheet of labels on which you hope to print. The size of the individual labels should be stated either on the sheet itself, or on the outer package. If it's not mentioned, measure a label carefully and note its size.

2. Measure the label page (usually A4) then measure top, bottom, side and central margins.

3.   Create shaded frames to represent all page margins, and move them into place.

4.   Create a frame which exactly mirrors the desired label, and give it a fine pale grey dotted line all around.

5.   Copy this frame onto the clipboard, then paste as many versions as the page needs, and move them into position on the page, butting right up to the shaded margin areas.

6.   Remove the shading from the margin areas, so that it doesn't print out.

Let's look at an example (Figure 21). The labels upon which we want to print are Avery No. L7165, a page of eight labels, each measuring 9.91cm x 6.77cm. The side margins measure 4mm each, and the central

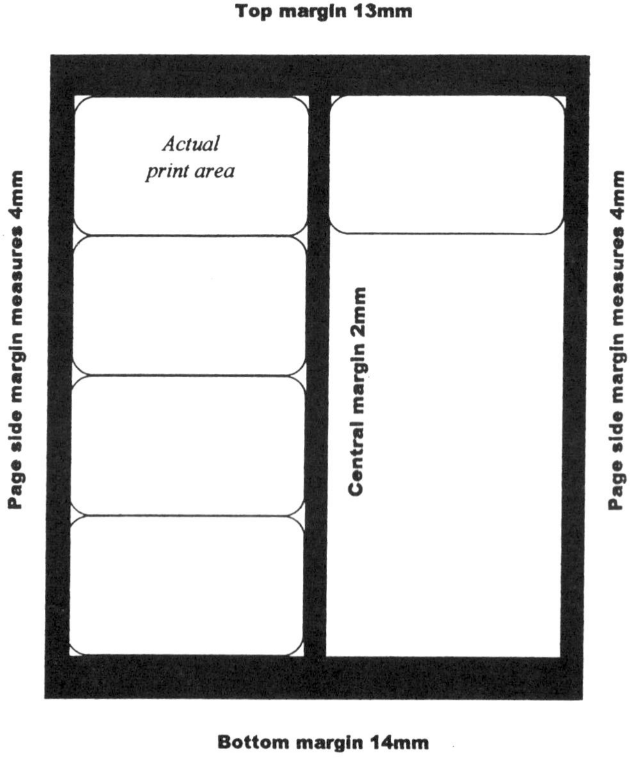

Fig. 21. An example page of labels, not to scale.

margin 2mm. Top and bottom margins on the page measure 13 and 14mm respectively.

Note that, on our example, the page does not include top and bottom margins around the labels themselves, and bears only a central margin. These margin allowances vary according to label size. If your finished 'label' does not fit onto the page the designated number of times, the chances are that you have more or less margin than you should have. Recheck your calculations.

Although this might sound complicated, you'll find it very simple when you've done it a couple of times. Make sure you save each label setting as a new, preferably code numbered file, or style template, so that you can input new label information into it each time.

LABELLING FOR GARDENERS

Ask most keen gardeners what their main preoccupations with regard to gardening are, and they'll almost certainly include 'labelling'. The plastic labels supplied by most nurseries and garden centres are fine as temporary measures, but they degrade very quickly and remove themselves from the pot with the least persuasion. Far stronger plastic and wooden labels are available, but trying to find a method of marking them permanently seems doomed to failure, as even those markers which advertise themselves as 'permanent' are permanent only when not faced with extremes of weather. Enterprising garden suppliers offer various solutions to the problem, such as 'scratch on' labels in a variety of materials, or attractive moulded terracotta labels, but these are very expensive for the gardener faced with labelling hundreds of plants.

The computer solution

There are at least two ways of dealing with this problem using your computer. Firstly, you can print 'standard plant label' sized stick-on labels which if printed according to instruction, will last far longer than marking pencil, so-called permanent marker, or the labelling used by most nurseries and garden centres. Secondly, you can print onto tractor fed soft plastic labels, which again, if printed according to instruction, will last and last.

The way to print these labels is to print using a dot matrix printer fitted with a *plasticised* rather than a fabric ribbon. The print produced by this kind of ribbon is weatherproof to a much greater degree than that produced using a fabric ribbon, and if allowed to 'set' into the label for a short time before use, will persist long after most other methods have been abandoned.

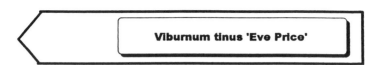

Fig. 22. A standard plant label complete with computer
produced 'stick-on' label.

The labels used must be of excellent quality if they are to stand up to the rigours of the British weather. Those I use are manufactured by Fisher Clark Limited, and are sold in packs of 12,000.

Soft plastic tractor-fed labels come in a variety of shapes and sizes and can be purchased from wholesale suppliers of computer peripherals. They come in sheets of 30 or 40 labels, depending upon size, and are perforated for easy removal from the page.

When producing such labels, we need to think about what the gardener actually wants. There are a number of ways of approaching the task. You could produce packs of say 500 labels, including the most popular shrubs, trees and perennials. However, it would make far more sense actually to ask gardeners what they want by advertising in the classified sections of gardening magazines. The readers will hopefully provide you with their wants, and you will respond accordingly.

An even more profitable method might be to contact either local gardening societies, or one of the many national gardening associations in the country. The Hardy Plant Society, for instance, has a national branch, plus many local and special interest branches, any or all of whom might be interested in your service.

Getting the information onto the page

If you are producing the kind of small labels which might be of interest to gardeners, the most efficient method would be to create a database of all plant names as you are asked for them, and then to select those which you currently require, to export into your document or software. Failing that, you are faced with the prospect of entering each one individually onto a pre-designed label.

Although this might sound daunting, most of the popular names would still need to be entered only once. It would then be a simple matter to save the pages of ready-to-print labels in logically named files, and to do some quick manipulation where perhaps three quarters of the page are required, and the rest are not, or are to be substituted with others from another page. Although this method would be more time consuming than using a database, intelligent use of grouped frames for copying across would minimise the amount of time spent creating the pages of labels.

ADDRESSING THE PROBLEM

There has been a steady growth in the number of organisations offering small gold and multi-coloured name and address labels to individuals over the last few years, so you might think that there is no additional market for such things. However, I'm pleased to say that you're wrong. Many of the existing small labels are not acceptable on the backs of cheques, because they are too heavy and threaten to gum up the computer at the bank. The same kind of labels we looked at for plant labelling, however, are perfect for the backs of cheques.

In addition, individuals welcome the chance to obtain larger sized name and address labels for inclusion on stamped addressed envelopes and so forth, as long as they are not too expensive. With labelling software, they are very quick and simple, and thus cheap, to produce, but even without the software they can be produced economically.

Producing company blanks

Using labelling software, word processing software or DTP, it's a simple job to produce blanks for local companies and organisations, which feature their name and address, complete with space for them to enter the addressee details. You can make them as plain or as fancy as you like, as long as the quality is good. Many organisations may not have thought of the possibility of having pre-printed mailing labels, but they make such a difference to the look of despatched goods that most organisations, when shown the possibilities, are keen to order. Let's produce a couple for the company featured on our database chapter (see Figure 23).

BOOKPLATES FOR BOOK LOVERS

The nicest thing about producing labels is that you can have fun! Bookplates can be produced either on labels or on card, which is then used as a book-mark. For most people, however, the most useful are those which can be stuck into books, so that should they be loaned out at any time, they are much more likely to find their way home, particularly if the wording on the bookplate is such that it nudges the conscience of the borrower. Take a look at the examples in Figure 24.

Marketing your bookplates

The most likely buyers of your bookplates are small local bookshops. I would suggest that you create samples printed onto sheets of good quality, preferably white, labels of a suitable size, and take them into your

This very simple example could be used at small to medium size for mailing letters, circulars etc, and sized up to provide mailing labels for larger packages.

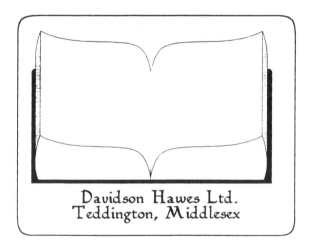

This example uses a graphic which represents the nature of the business carried on by Davidson Hawes Ltd. Any graphic can be used as long as it can be adapted to fit the task, in this case, to provide the necessary space for the addressee.

Fig. 23. Examples of company 'blanks'.

THIS BOOK

FITS PERFECTLY
INTO THE BOOKCASE OF

_____

_____
loves this book.
Please send it home.

Thank you!

Fig. 24. Bookplates to nudge the conscience.

Fig. 25. Preserve labels.

chosen bookshops. If the bookshop is chary about taking stocks, ask if they will take a small sample selection to see how they sell.

When producing the packs of bookplates, you could either produce single design packs of, say, 12-20 individual plates, carefully cut, or you could package them in sheets. Either way, pack neatly into clear plastic bags, create a product label which will show through the plastic, and pack the labels at the back of the package facing outwards, so that the potential buyer can see the design. Make sure that your prices are competitive, allowing for capital costs, your profit and for the shop's mark-up, which may well be 30 per cent or more.

DESIGNING FOR LOCAL ORGANISATIONS

By local organisations I'm thinking principally of local charities, the Women's Institute, in fact any organisation which produces **goods for sale**. Whilst we might like to think that packaging is of little importance, it is in fact paramount, which is why companies go to such lengths to design and produce attractive packaging for their products. This is just as true for the local WI as it is for giant multi-nationals.

Think about the kinds of products produced for sale by such small organisations, and see if you can come up with labelling ideas which might suit. The obvious example for the WI is jam-making. What sort of labels could you produce which might help sell produce of this sort?

Figure 25 will give you just some idea of the possibilities of selling through local organisations. Don't they look more tempting than the plain hand-written labels often seen on such produce? If you don't fancy contacting the WI, how about designing wine bottle labels for home-made wine buffs? They could be sold through local suppliers of wine making equipment, through wine circles, or even through your local newspaper via the small ads column. The possibilities for such output are vast; all it takes is a little imagination and the courage to approach the organisation concerned.

MAKING 'MOVING DAY' A LITTLE LESS FRAUGHT

Finally in this chapter, I want to look at producing labels designed to help with the horrendous chore of moving house. If you have moved house in the last few years, you'll know that the old tea chests have largely gone, to be replaced by cardboard cartons which feature printed-on boxes which allow you to detail the room in which the box should be put, the contents of the box, and any other information which might be of use.

This diagram represents an A4 page, which is divided into two A5 portions, each contains a label. If we chose bright green for the dining room, the removal men would quickly learn that anything with a green label is for that room, and anything with any other colour label is for another room. The labels can be attached to cartons, or to pieces of furniture.

In this example, in addition to choosing a different colour, we've added the optional information that the contents are fragile, in the hope that the removal men will handle the carton with care. The information included can be for the benefit of the householder, the removal men, or both, so for example, where the package contains books from a particular bookcase, the label could say so, to help organise unpacking.

Fig. 26. Housemove labels.

Whilst this sounds as though it should be a good idea, the sad fact is that the spaces allotted to the information are tiny, and the boxes all look the same, so the chances are that whatever information is in the box, the carton will end up in the wrong place. For householders with lots of china, books, CDs *etc* to pack and unpack, this can mean a nightmare once they actually get into the new home, as boxes will be piled on top of boxes, with no way of telling what is in each.

The solution

The solution is a simple one, and one in which many local removal firms might show an interest. You will need to obtain a mixed pack of brightly coloured A4 paper; as many different colours as possible, or failing this, buy small separate packs. Buy reasonable weight paper, and if you can find self-adhesive, so much the better.

The idea is to design large labels, using large text, detailing the room into which each item of furniture, or each box, will go. These labels will then be printed onto different coloured paper.

Labels for where?

With most houses, you'll need the following labels: Kitchen, Sitting Room or Lounge, Dining Room, Bedroom 1, Bedroom 2, Bedroom 3. Add optional labels for Study, Bedroom 4 and beyond, Bathroom(s), Cloakroom, Garage, various outbuildings, and any other rooms you can think of. This tells you how many different colours you need to find. The idea of colour coding in this way is that the removal men will very quickly realise that if the dining room boxes are green, any other colour shouldn't be there. Labels will be placed so that they show both on the top of the box, and on the front, *ie* they should be folded, then taped both to the top, and to the front. That way, their eventual destination is much easier to spot.

Figure 26 shows some designs.

To speed up placement of goods into the new home even further, you could provide A4 labels of matching text and colour to put on the door of each room so that the removal men know instantly which room is which.

Marketing your housemove labels

The real point about these housemove labels is that they benefit both removal men and householder, so you could target both. To target removal men, send local firms a small sample pack. Include a bright and breezy leaflet explaining how the system would work and how it would benefit removal men, particularly in terms of time and thus money saved, then sit back and wait for orders. However, be prepared to cope with large orders for the more popular rooms, and make sure you can source the paper in the required number of colours.

To target householders, place a small ad in the 'Property for Sale' column of your local paper. Give a telephone number or address where you can be contacted, then send enquirers one or two sheets, accompanied by your leaflet, this time explaining the benefits to householders. This might be the best way to start, as quantities of paper will not be so great.

Pricing

The price of packs should reflect the cost of the paper, overheads such as advertising, your time and effort, *and* your profit. Where you supply bulk packs, let the price reflect the fact that you might be able to buy the paper cheaper in bulk, but be careful about offering credit to removal firms until you're sure that you can organise your cash flow efficiently. In the early days at least, ask for cash with order. With individual householders, it is preferable to stick with cash with order terms.

CHECKLIST

● Look at any labelling facilities offered by your word processing software and see if they can be adapted to your labelling needs. If not, examine the process of creating your own page of labels.

● Look around at the various qualities and prices of label on offer. Most suppliers charge the recommended price, but see if you can find a supplier, perhaps mail order, offering discounts on larger quantities.

● The only problem with the housemove labels featured is that self adhesive brightly coloured labels are difficult to find, so we end up using coloured paper instead. Investigate the various methods of sticking these coloured sheets onto cartons, as you may be called upon to advise either householders or removal firms buying your product.

CASE STUDIES

Brian and his 'Chequemates'

When Brian first looked at the possibilities of producing labels, he decided to use a small photographic transparency labelling program he had bought some years previously to produce name and address labels for the backs of cheques. These labels (11mm x 70mm) fit perfectly across the backs of cheques, and save cheque users having to write out their name and address each time. Brian was pleased to discover that, in spite of the fact that more and more people are using debit cards instead of cheques, the sales of his 'Chequemates' were very encouraging.

Andrew has another brainwave

Being the proud owner of the latest version of the most popular labelling program, Andrew decided to offer a variety of labels to appeal to young people, including audio tape labels, A4 file binder labels, and of all things, over-the-top wacky bedroom or flat door labels, made from 'Dayglo' coloured papers, and incorporating the weirdest of images. The first two ideas fell flat with the exception of one or two orders, but his door labels took off, particularly as his charges were relatively low. His ex and current student friends ended up vying with each other for the most extreme labels, so Andrew was able both to use his designing skills to the full and to make a considerable profit on the venture.

Alison kicks herself . . .

Because she never thought of it before. She was already producing a wide variety of letter heads, comp slips *etc* for local firms for whom she worked, so it was a simple task to set her system up to produce mailing labels in a variety of sizes. Too many firms, she decided, sent out goods with scruffy hand written addresses, never thinking of the bad impression created at the receiving end. With her help, she told herself, these firms could be saved from the effects of their own inattention to detail.

DISCUSSION POINTS

1. If you were asked to supply a local removal firm with bulk packs of housemove labels, how would you go about producing them?

2. What local charities or organisations are there in your area which might be able to use produce labels? What about farm shops or similar, which perhaps at present use crudely produced hand written labels; could you offer them your services?

3. Could you 'do an Andrew' and dream up some weird and wonderful uses for labels? Do you have access to the kinds of people who might welcome your ideas? Local schools and colleges might offer the best bet. Look again at Chapter 2 and the advice on advertising on college notice boards.

9
Selling Your Knowledge

ADVISING BEGINNERS

Can you remember how you felt the first time you sat down in front of a computer? Chances are you were petrified, if a little excited, and thought that if you touched it, or pressed the wrong key, it might blow up, or worse. That's how most new computer owners feel. They find themselves sitting in front of this monster which until now, they really wanted – and realising that in fact they don't want it at all. They wish it would disappear in a puff of blue smoke, and give them their money back.

This is where you come in. Not you and your computer this time, but you and your expertise. After all, you're an old hand now. Total beginners need someone like you to hold their hand for a day or two until they get the hang of things. But don't imagine these jobs will last, because they won't. Once your client has the feel of his or her machine, they'll want you out of the way, so that they can play. That's fine, as long as they know that you're there, in the background, should problems arise.

Letting them know you exist

Probably the simplest way to let beginners know of your services is to ask local computer retailers to advertise or advise of your service for a small percentage of any money you earn. However, many people buy their computers mail order, so you'll miss out on a large sector by doing only that. Combine approaches by placing small ads in the 'Computers for sale' column of your local paper. That way you stand a much greater chance of contacting more of the people who need you.

You can't expect to charge a great deal for this service, but whatever you decide to charge, make sure that you stress *plus expenses* as you'll probably inevitably be involved in travelling to and from the premises of your client.

What will you teach?

Those who have bought their computers locally will often find that the

102

retailer will set up the system upon delivery, and will give them a brief overview of Windows, Dos and possibly any other software they've purchased. However, that overview will have been *very* brief, so ask how you can help, and act accordingly.

If Windows is a foreign language, talk them through the basics, then leave them to find their way around. If they'd like specific help with software, ask which program it is, and if you know it, all well and good. If, however, it's something new to you, tread carefully. If it's the kind of software you've dealt with in another package – word processing, or accounting for instance – you might well be able to generalise your knowledge from those you know. Look around the software to familiarise yourself with it, then sit with the client and work through the tutorial together, so that your client learns a little of what the program can do.

Using the manual
Don't suggest to your client that he or she should read the accompanying manual before tackling the software. Many software manuals might as well have been written in a foreign language for all the use they are to beginners – they are invariably written by experienced programmers, and thus unwittingly assume a knowledge which the beginner does not have. Suggest instead that your client read the manual whilst sitting in front of the computer, so that the information in the manual can be applied to the software on the screen. That way, it will make much more sense.

If you find yourself faced with software you've never seen before, don't waste both your and your client's time by pretending that you can quickly get to grips with it. Admit your lack of knowledge now, rather than having to extricate yourself later, after you've drawn both you and your client into a hopeless muddle.

How will you teach?
Don't alienate your clients by talking down to them, or by being patronising, just because you know more about computers than they do. After all, they might be expert in astronomy or taxonomy or a whole host of other subject areas about which you know nothing. Be patient and understanding, and talk as though talking to an intelligent and well respected relative.

TEACHING AT LEISURE CLASSES

'Leisure' classes are those classes run by local authorities which offer a huge variety of interest areas, usually at night schools, but sometimes during the day and, increasingly, at fortnight long 'summer schools'. Their aim is largely to teach at beginner and intermediate levels, although some offer advanced level courses leading to full time courses and qualifications.

Lecturers at these courses are those who can display a fair degree of expertise in their chosen subject, and the potential to teach that subject. They do not necessarily have to have formal qualifications, as they are generally paid considerably less than their qualified colleagues.

Looking at courses on offer

Although local authorities vary considerably, the subjects on offer generally include those which (a) have a ready supply of available teachers, and (b) are likely to be of interest to a wide variety of people. Computer subjects are usually broken down into very narrow areas, so that if you can display the necessary proficiency in just one word processing package, you might well be considered for that subject. However, it's no use being proficient in a package which came out with Babbage's first computer. Such dinosaurs do not guarantee full classes. Authorities like to fill the classroom in order to make running the course financially worthwhile, so you have to be offering a well-known and well-used product.

Making yourself known as a potential teacher

To enquire about the possibilities of teaching at leisure classes, either contact the local authority education department direct, or wait until they advertise their needs in the local press. I'd advise the former, as by the time their notices appear you may well find that your particular niche has been filled.

SETTING UP SYSTEMS FOR SMALL BUSINESSES

Just as individual newcomers to computers are often at a loss to know where to begin, so are new business users, who often have to face the physical setting up and configuration of their computers, printers, scanners *etc* before they can start looking into the possibilities of the newly bought system.

Maximising your chances

If you can get in before this stage, and advise upon the *purchase* of their system, even better. Beginners in business computing, faced with the minefield of the computer supply industry, will welcome unbiased information about the kind of hardware and software most likely to meet their requirements. However, don't be tempted to get into this unless you really are up-to-date with the market. Computer technology changes so fast that computers are out of date before they are even out of their boxes!

Setting up hardware components

If you are *au fait* with connecting computers, printers, printer selectors, UPS units and so forth, you can combine *this* service with installing and setting up software. That can then be followed up with teaching the software to what will often be inexperienced users. As you might guess, this can be a very lucrative field indeed, particularly where you are able to offer follow-up consultation services as problems arise. Such contracts may well offer a regular income for a number of months, especially where you're dealing in a specialised market.

Finding your clients

Again, to find your clients, ask local computer retailers to advertise your services for a percentage or a flat fee. Even more profitably, see if you can talk these retailers into adopting you as their set-up representative, so that anyone with problems is referred to you. Again, you'd have to give them a percentage of your proceeds, but you may well find yourself earning considerable sums as a result of their efforts.

Advertising your presence

It's also worth advertising locally, but make sure your advertising targets the right people. Choose the day your local paper runs its 'Small Business' section, and advertise in that, using display or semi display. Better still, see if you can persuade the paper to feature you and your services in an 'advertising feature'. This is a feature which includes details and copy about the chosen business, either free of charge or for a small fee.

It might also be worth producing a press release to send out to local newspapers and your local radio station. This more speculative approach often works where other methods fail, particularly where your targets are short of copy to fill a particular slot.

QUESTIONS AND ANSWERS

I quite like the idea of teaching newcomers, but I'm afraid I'd be terribly nervous. What do you suggest I do to overcome such fears?
I fully accept that approaching something entirely new can be quite nerve wracking, but I'd suggest that once you've made the first move, and found your first 'pupil', the simple fact that you are, so to speak, the

Selling your knowledge to beginners

Talking individuals through
initial set-up and familiarisation
of hardware

Teaching beginners at day and
evening leisure classes

↓

↓

Advising upon suitable software

Teaching at Summer Schools

↓

↘ ↙

Talking through basics of
operating systems

Note that this could involve
you in teaching of a variety
of software packages, provided
you can avoid timetable clashes

↓

↓

Teaching chosen software

Offering later one-to-one
teaching and support sessions
(but check that your contract
allows this)

↓

Offering technical and/or
software support in the
event of later problems

*The more you can combine the two columns, the more your potential
earnings, but don't offer to teach at Leisure classes until you are sure
you have mastered the craft of effective teaching.*

Fig. 27. Selling your knowledge to beginners.

Selling your knowledge to small businesses

Advising on purchase of ◄──► Advising on suitable
hardware systems   software

Installing and setting up   Installing software
operating systems

Setting up local networks ──► Organising site licences for
                                 network users

Teaching potential users the   Talking new users through the
basics of computer and printer   software, to get them started
use

Offering support services on   Offering full scale teaching of
a 'consultancy' basis, either   software, to fully familiarise
to deal with problems as they   users
arise, or to advise on later
system enhancements

                                 Offering support services on a
                                 'consultancy' basis, both to deal
                                 with problems as they arise,
                                 and to advise on additional
                                 'bolt-ons'.

Consultancy in both fields has the potential
to lead to further lucrative opportunities.

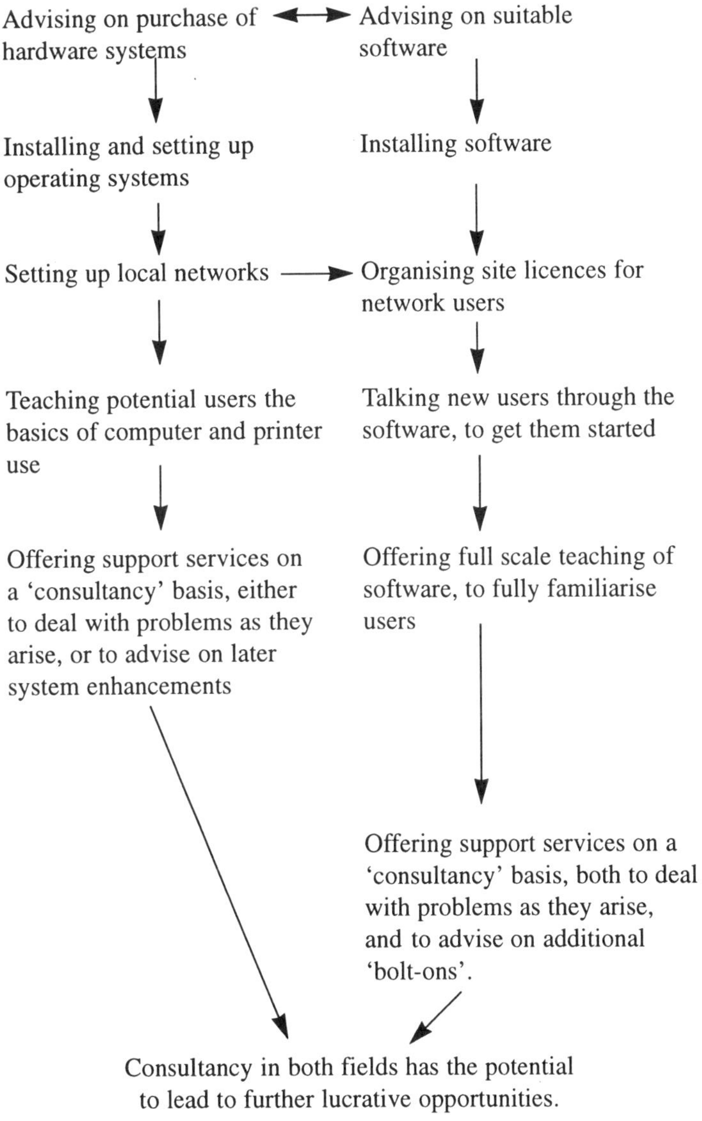

*Looking at the above, you'll see that where you enter the equation will
be dictated by your technical expertise. The nearer the top your entry
point, and the more you can combine both columns, the higher your
potential earnings.*

Fig. 28. Selling your knowledge to small businesses.

one with power in the situation will enable you to forget your nerves. Don't think of your potential clients as people who are waiting to catch you out on what you don't know, think of them rather as people who will be really grateful for the help you are able to offer them. One or two successes will build your self confidence, and I'm sure you'll soon find yourself wondering what all the fuss was about.

You mentioned a 'press release' earlier. What is it, and how do I go about producing one?
A 'press release' is a notice combining advertising and news, which is circulated to any potentially interested bodies who might publicise its contents. To be effective, *ie* to be sure of being used, a press release must give the appearance at least of containing items of real news or information in which readers of the target publications might be interested. However, skilled producers are often able to combine that information with 'plugs' for their company or product, and thus gain what is effectively 'free' advertising. Many companies, large and small, use press releases to augment their advertising budgets.

Producing an effective press release is a skill which can be learned. Study the relevant chapter in a book about advertising, or better still, read Peter Bartram's excellent *How to Write a Press Release* in this series.

This question is related to the earlier one, about nervousness in teaching. I really think I'm knowledgeable enough to teach at leisure classes, but I've never taught a class, and I don't know whether I'd actually be able to control a room full of people.
The nice thing about teaching leisure classes is that those attending are there because they want to be, not because they have to be. They have chosen their subject and have paid for the privilege of attending. That means of course that, for the most part, control doesn't come into it. In well organised classes, each student will have their own computer, so their attention will be focused upon that and upon what you are saying. The overwhelming feeling at most classes I've attended has been one of fun. The people there have enjoyed their learning, as with just a little knowledge, and some practice, they find they come on leaps and bounds.

Don't be afraid of tackling leisure classes. They really are very enjoyable, and very rewarding, and I don't mean just in the financial sense.

CHECKLIST

● Take a fresh look at the software you know best, and decide how you would go about teaching someone who had never seen it before. Think about how to structure your teaching so that your pupil will learn progressively. Think also about how you might monitor your pupil's progress, so that you don't go on to a new subject area before the current one has been properly mastered.

- See if you can find out what computer-based leisure classes are being offered in your area. Put together a package based upon your own specialist area, and send it to the authority in question, in an attempt to persuade them that you are the person to teach any course(s) not currently on offer.

- Even if you consider yourself to be well up in the market, buy a couple of current computer magazines, and familiarise yourself with the latest in both hardware and software. What is the current 'entry level' for hardware systems, and how do prices vary as systems become more powerful?

CASE STUDIES

Brian's first day at 'school'

As Brian had considerable experience at managing people, he decided that he could profitably use his expertise to teach computerised book-keeping at night classes. He contacted his local education authority, who were delighted to welcome him onto their team because of his qualifications and wide experience.

Before his first session, Brian prepared a teaching programme which incorporated the basics of book-keeping for those who had no experience. He had expected to find that at least some of his students would be complete novices, but was pleased to discover that all had at least some experience of manual systems.

Brian's biggest problem was that he wasn't a natural teacher, he had a tendency to assume a certain level of knowledge in his students, and found himself resenting the fact that he had to explain so many of what he considered to be basic principles. After a chat with the leisure classes organiser, during which he was encouraged to talk about his difficulties, he realised the mistake he was making and agreed to give teaching another try.

It took Brian some time to adjust to his new role, but as his class progressed he realised that he had something of real value to offer. The feedback from his pupils was very positive; they found Brian's obvious expertise and confidence in his subject of real benefit.

Andrew is already teaching, in an unpaid capacity

Because of his enthusiasm and general air of knowledge, Andrew had always found himself called upon to explain this, or to sort out that, even sometimes helping his teachers out when they encountered problems. However, although he enjoyed the role in an unofficial capacity, he doubted his ability to carry it off officially. He felt that to some extent, his age was against him and that he was too lately a student himself to switch roles to become a tutor. Also, he felt that signing up for a term of night school classes might be tricky because the timing might interfere with his starting at university.

Alison talks to the press

Alison decided that in order to optimise her chances of selling her services as a software instructor, she would approach the local newspaper, talk to them about how successful her advertising with them had been, and ask them to help her spread her wings a little.

The paper offered to include a piece in their Business section, and even agreed to a photograph. Alison produced the copy, which of course the paper edited, but in spite of their slight distortion of the facts, she found herself inundated with requests for help.

With so many possibilities on offer, Alison was able to pick and choose, so selected two clients who required teaching at the weekend, which meant that she could continue with her other work.

DISCUSSION POINTS

1. Although in theory Brian started out the right way, he found his inbuilt attitudes were a bar to progress in his teaching. What advice would you give to Brian to help him overcome the problem he encountered?

2. Do you think Andrew was right in avoiding a formal teaching situation? Was his youth necessarily a bar to good relationships, and thus results, with students?

3. Alison was very daring in her approach, and it paid dividends. How would you go about persuading the editor of your local paper, or a local radio station, that you were worth their time and attention?

10
Understanding Your Tax Position

FACING THE FACT OF INCOME TAX

At some point during your new career, you will have to face the unpalatable fact that you are earning above the threshold for *income tax*. You may be earning solely from your computer, or you may have combined earnings, either from one or more jobs or from 'unearned income' coming in as interest on investments or savings. It may even be a combination of all those factors.

Whatever the source of your income, I cannot stress too strongly that when you reach the point at which the Chancellor decides you should pay income tax, you must contact your local tax office so that you can be assessed for tax. Grim though that may sound, the alternative – being caught out by the Inland Revenue – is even worse. You could be subject to heavy fines, imprisonment or both. The completion of tax returns may seem like a nightmare, but it is considerably less of a nightmare than being locked up at Her Majesty's pleasure.

Obviously, given that there are whole books written on the subject of tax, I can give only a brief overview of the system as it applies to your earnings and allowable expenses. For more detailed information, turn to one of the excellent tax guides produced annually by various institutions, and available from any good book shop.

For our immediate purposes, I am going to assume that you are working on a 'self-employed' basis (you cannot simply assert that you are self-employed – the tax inspector has to agree that you are in business on your own account) and that you are earning solely by working with your computer.

KEEPING EFFICIENT RECORDS

In order that you can be properly assessed for tax purposes, you *must* keep **accurate records** of all incomings, ie earnings, and all outgoings. With the introduction of self assessment for tax, it is a legal requirement that all such records should be properly maintained, and must be kept for a period of five years. You should also retain those documents relating to your records, such as invoices, so that they can be produced should the Inland Revenue ask for them. Failure to adhere to these requirements can result in fines of up to £3,000.

Setting expenses against tax

One of the benefits of keeping efficient records of outgoings is that a proportion of such expenses, provided they are wholly and exclusively for your business, is allowable against tax. There are no definitive rules about what is and what is not allowable; each case is judged on its merits, but if you can show that an expense is justified, as a general rule it will be allowed against tax. These are the kinds of expenses which may well be allowable:

- advertising

- computer software, where bought separately from your computer

- books, magazines and professional subscriptions where these are directly related to your business

- travelling expenses

- the VAT paid on purchases used for your business (this ceases to be the case should you ever decide to become registered for VAT)

- postage and printing charges

- a *proportion of* operating expenses such as heating, lighting and telephone costs

- accountancy fees should you become involved in them.

  Expenses which are **not** allowable are:

- normal living expenses

- most of your National Insurance contributions, but see section on Class 4 contributions

- initial cost of capital equipment, *eg* computer hardware.

Capital expenditure

You will have noticed that computer hardware is not included in the 'allowable' list. This is because it is treated as capital equipment, for which capital allowances can be claimed. Capital allowances are calculated differently from business expenses in that you can claim only a proportion of the cost of such assets each year, setting that figure against profits. Different rules apply to different capital assets, but for our purposes we'll assume that your computer, printer, photocopier and whatever else you use for your business are in one 'pool of expenditure' as it is called. Currently, you are allowed to set 25 per cent of the total cost of that pool against tax each year.

Let's look at an example:

Capital item	Purchase price
Desktop computer	£1,100.00
Laptop computer	£1,400.00
Dot matrix printer	£225.00
Inkjet printer	£270.00
Computer workstation	£95.00
Photocopier	£470.00
Total value of pool	**£3,560.00**
Set against profit (25%)	£890.00
'Written down' value carried over to future years	£2,670.00

The amount carried over can be set against tax in future years, at the rate of 25 per cent of the reducing written down value each year. If any item from the pool is sold during that time, its value must be deducted from the total before capital allowances for the year are calculated. The amount deducted is the smaller of either the original cost of the asset or the money received from the sale. In certain circumstances, the sale of an asset could give rise to what is called a 'balancing charge', or a 'balancing allowance', resulting in an adjustment to your taxable profit for the year. Consult your chosen tax guide for further information.

PERSONAL ALLOWANCES

In addition to those items of expenditure which are allowable against tax, each individual has their personal allowance which differs according to circumstances. These allowances are the same for self employed people as they are for employees paying under PAYE.

At the time of writing, these allowances are as follows:

Under 65 years	
Personal allowance (single person)	£3,765
Married couple's allowance	£1,790
Additional personal allowance (eg single parent)	£1,790
65-74 years	
Personal allowance	£4,910
Married couple's allowance	£3,155

In addition to the above basic allowances, there are of course others which individuals may claim, for instance, mortgage interest relief, charity donations *etc*. For more guidance, ask your tax office for a copy of leaflet IR90 – *Tax allowances and reliefs*.

There is also some flexibility in the way that the married couple's allowance is treated, now that married couples can be assessed separately for tax (see leaflet IR80).

Calculating the amount of tax you'll pay

The amount of tax you end up paying is arrived at by combining your personal allowance with however much you are claiming in the way of operating expenses and capital allowances. Tax on the remainder will be paid at the prevailing rates, currently:

20% on taxable income up to	....	£3,900
24% on taxable income between £3,900 and	....	£25,500
40% on all taxable income over £25,500	....	

An instant tax advantage

The one bright spot on the horizon regarding tax is that, as a self-employed person, you will normally be expected to pay tax at the end of the financial year, rather than on a Pay As You Earn basis. What this means in practice is that there is a considerable delay in earning money and paying tax on it. Although you must budget for the tax you'll have to pay, the money can be earning for you in an interest bearing account until your tax demand appears.

Being treated as a freelance

If, perhaps because of your other commitments, your income is seasonal or irregular, the Inland Revenue may prefer to treat you as a freelance, rather than as a self-employed person. This normally means that you will pay tax on a current year basis *ie* that the tax inspector will base his assessment of your income upon what you earned in the previous year, and will tax accordingly.

PAYING NATIONAL INSURANCE

As a self-employed person, you may have to pay National Insurance contributions. Most self employed people pay flat rate Class 2 contributions, although some have to pay Class 4 where their earnings are above a certain rate. NI contributions used to be paid weekly, via the purchase of a stamp from the Post Office. Since April 1993, however, they have been paid either by monthly direct debit through a bank or building society, or by the direct payment of quarterly bills. Payment of Class 2 contributions normally gives access to the following basic benefits:

● sickness benefit

● invalidity or incapacity benefit

● maternity allowance

● retirement pension

● widow's benefit where the contributor is a married man.

The do **not** however, entitle you to unemployment benefit, except under certain exceptional circumstances, to industrial injuries benefit, or to additional earnings-related amounts on top of basic pension or widow's benefits.

If your earnings are below the threshold for NI contributions (currently £3,430) and you expect them to stay that way, you can obtain a certificate of exception. For further information, see leaflet N127 at your local Social Security Office. However, you should bear in mind that non-payment of NI contributions will affect some of your entitlement to benefits.

Paying Class 4 National Insurance

If your Taxable income *before allowances* exceeds a certain amount (currently £6,490) you will be expected to pay Class 4 contributions, which are earnings-related and are paid at the same time as your income tax bill. You should note, however, that the stated amount refers only to income from your self-employed business, it does not apply to income from investments. Class 4 contributions have no additional bearings on those benefits you might claim, but you can set 50 per cent of their cost against tax. For further details, see leaflet NI18, *Class 4 National Insurance Contributions* at your local Social Security Office.

QUESTIONS AND ANSWERS

The more I read about tax and National Insurance, the more confused I become. Can't I just bury my head and pretend it doesn't exist?
Actually, yes you can, but only if your earnings are, and will remain, very low. If you want to limit yourself this way, that's up to you, but it would make far more sense to get to grips with tax and NI. If you can't cope with it yourself, search out someone who can, and don't be afraid to ask the tax office for help. They produce an enormous amount of leaflets which are designed to help people like yourself, for whom such matters seem like a foreign language. As far as National Insurance is concerned, as long as you don't earn above the stated amount, you'll pay flat rate contributions, which alter only when the Chancellor alters the rate, so these are not difficult to sort out.

With regard to National Insurance, aren't there special rates for married women?
Yes and no. If you were a married woman or a widow on 6 April 1977, you could opt to pay reduced rate Class 1 contributions. However, the last date to take up this option was May 1977. Married women paying at these rates cannot claim retirement pension on their own contributions, but should be able to claim on their husband's contributions. It's worth noting, however, that some women paying these reduced rates may find themselves actually paying more than if they were paying at the standard rate. Leaflet NI1 *National Insurance for married women* gives further details.

When you say I should keep efficient and accurate records of all outgoings and incomings, do you actually mean I would keep proper accounts?
In essence, yes I do, although these accounts will not have to be forwarded to the Inland Revenue unless your turnover is in excess of £15,000. Below this amount, you need to produce what are called 'three-line' accounts, which show your sales, purchases and expenses, and net profits. These much simplified accounts do not mean, however, that you

need to be any less diligent about keeping careful records; in the event that your tax inspector wishes to examine your accounts more closely, you must be able to back them up with evidence.

CHECKLIST

- Have a look at the various tax guides which are published annually, and decide which one might be the most suitable for you. Bear in mind that some are produced for the lay reader and others for the professional.

- Create a 'pool of expenditure' for yourself by documenting the cost of your computer hardware and any other relevant items such as your photocopier or work station. Locate the invoices for these items if you can, and create a file in which they may be safely held until the time when you'll be able to charge them against tax.

- Create a model system of accounts, detailing mythical incomings and outgoings, keeping it as simple as possible. Create another file, this time for the safe keeping of invoices for peripherals such as paper, ink cartridges and floppy disks. Establish a numerical or alphabetical system which will allow instant access to any of these items should they be required by your tax inspector.

CASE STUDIES

Brian ponders paying higher rate tax

Brian's earnings consist of a combination of company pension, investment income and the income earned from his various endeavours since being made redundant. He has been very successful in the various areas he's entered, but is concerned about the possibility of going over the threshold for higher rate tax as this would considerably affect not only his earned income, but also his investment and pension income.

Regrettably, he was forced to curtail some of his activities, because he recognised that becoming liable for higher rate tax would make him considerably worse off. He decided therefore to pursue only those jobs which he found enjoyable, such as teaching and book-keeping. Word-processing work had anyway tailed off because of his other commitments, and he found CV production less satisfactory than much of his other work. His biggest regret was that he would have to cut down on DTP, as this, although most enjoyable, was his biggest earner, and the one most likely to push him over the limit.

Andrew ponders paying *any* tax

Andrew was earning steadily from his various endeavours, but he didn't want the hassle of dealing with tax and National Insurance. Also, because he'd never imagined that he would be so successful, he had never bothered keeping any of his invoices, which he knew he'd need if he was to claim against purchases.

Because he lives with his parents, who were happy to supplement his living expenses, he decided to limit the amount of work he took in, particularly in view of the fact that he would soon be off to university. He knew that once he went off to study he'd have little time to supplement his grant, because he'd simply be too busy.

Alison – liable for tax at last

Alison had long dreamed of earning enough to do more than keep body and soul together, so she wasn't thrown by the fact that she was earning well above the rates both for income tax and for National Insurance. With two children to support, she was pleased that her National Insurance contributions would mean she could claim sickness benefit in the event of illness, and also that they would go towards a pension.

Thanks to her book-keeping activities, she found keeping her own accounts easy, although she had a tendency to ignore the fact that it needed doing each month, because of the pressure of other, paying, work. However, a run-in with the tax inspector over a missing invoice soon persuaded her that she would be much better served if she organised herself properly, and devoted a set time each month to the maintenance of her accounts.

DISCUSSION POINTS

1. Even if you have never considered it before, look now at your position regarding tax. How might you minimise your tax burden in the event of additional earnings?

2. In our case studies, Brian was forced to relinquish some of his roles in order to remain beneath the threshold for Higher Rate tax. If you were faced with that situation, how would you balance enjoyment of a particular field with the need to reduce earnings?

3. Because Alison is a single parent, she is entitled to extra allowances. Are there any special circumstances which might be to *your* advantage from a taxation point of view?

And Finally . . .

In this book I've sought to deal with the most popular and accessible areas for earning with your computer. However, there are areas I haven't covered, including spreadsheet techniques and Computer Aided Design (CAD), both of which I feel are probably too technical for general users. I've also omitted many other, more specialised, applications.

When you are confident in using your computer as a tool for earning, you might consider more specialised areas such as garden design, graphic design, dedicated photograph enhancement, and the use of databases in the setting up of pen-pal, introduction, and other agencies.

If you become involved with the Internet, there are high paying opportunities for those able to write home pages, using HTML (hypertext mark-up language), plus I have no doubt, a whole host of other opportunities, which will reveal themselves in time to those who are open to them.

I wish you well in your endeavours.

Glossary

Allowable expenses. Business expenses which are allowable against taxable profits.

Back up copy. A compressed copy of computer files, usually saved onto floppy disks, which can be retrieved in the event of file loss due to system failure.

Capital expenditure. That money which is spent on capital goods for a business, *i.e.*, goods which are necessary for the running of the business.

Combined approach package. The production of two or three related items, all of which incorporate aspects of a chosen design.

Curriculum Vitae. A resume of a person's career history to date, the aim of which is to give a potential employer an idea of an applicant's capabilities.

CV Profile. A short introduction to a CV, giving brief details of the applicant.

CV Skills analysis. The section in a CV which gives a brief overview of an applicant's professional abilities.

Database. A system for computerised storage, sorting, and retrieval of information.

DTP. Desk Top Publishing. The use of computers to design and produce publications.

Dummy. A mock-up, or invented design, produced to demonstrate the potential of a product.

File import/export. The import/export of a compatible file or files from one piece of software to another.

Floppy disk. A small portable disk, capable of storing small quantities of computer information.

Formatting. (In DTP and word processing). The application of layout guidelines to be used in the production of documents.

gsm. Grammes per square metre. Used in defining paper weights, and thus, uses.

Hardware. A computing term meaning the electronic and mechanical components of a computer system.

House Style. The general adoption of certain formatting rules which dictate the look of company publications.

Information field. A database software term meaning the section of a database into which chosen classes of information will be put.

Inkjet printer. A type of printer which produces its image by squirting millions of tiny jets of ink onto paper.

Jargon. Specialised terminology. Most fields of interest or specialist groups have their own jargon, which is intended to ensure shared meaning within the group.

Laser printer. A type of printer which uses highly refined photocopier technology to produce its image. This kind of printer gives the best results, but is expensive to buy and use.

Leading. Pronounced "ledding", this is a printing term meaning the space between lines of text.

Leisure Classes. Those local authority evening and other classes which are aimed mainly at hobbyists.

Multi-books. A version of accounting software which enables the user to operate the books of multiple companies.

Multi-user. A version of software which enables multiple users from the same loading of software, via a local network. This usually involves the purchase of a 'site license' for a given number of users.

Network. The 'joining' of a group of computers, so that each accesses a 'central pool' of software, called a 'file server'. The term 'local network' refers to a network of computers within an office or building, as distinct from an 'area' network across several buildings, cities, or even, countries.

Page design. The overall look and feel of a page, taking into account text, graphics, and space.

Personal allowance. Statutory allowances such as 'Single Person's', which are set against tax.

Press Release. A document containing news and/or information about a company, which is designed to facilitate free advertising.

Relational database. The kind of database which enables linkage of one database area to another, allowing full cross referencing of information.

Software. The 'enabling' aspect of a computer system, which allows users to operate their computers for chosen tasks.

Template. A measured-up outline, used to place text/graphics in the correct place for printing out onto a pre-formatted or designed sheet.

Voluntary Registration. The voluntary registration for VAT of a company whose annual turnover falls below that which requires compulsory registration.

White space. Literally, the space on a page surrounding text and/or graphics, which enables them to be seen and understood more readily.

Work station. A chosen place of work made up to incorporate most if not all of the various entities required for the job.

Useful Addresses

Data Protection Registar, Springfield House, Water Lane, Wilmslow, Chesire SK9 5AX. Tel: (01625) 535777.

The National Back Pain Association, 16 Elmtree Road, Teddington, Middlesex TW11 8ST. Tel: (0181) 977 5475. Produce an excellent series of booklets on all aspects of back care.

Avery Dennison, Gardner Road, Maidenhead, Berkshire SL6 7PU. Tel: 0800 805020. Producers of Avery 'LablePro®' labelling software and a vast range of labels suitable for virtually all office uses. They also have a Freephone telephone helpline (number as above) which offers free formatting guides for most word processing programs in use in Britain today (call them before you set about designing your own label pages, as they may well be able to save you the bother). They also offer free technical advice, formatting disks and label samples.

Fisher Clark (Label Manufacturers), Horncastle Road, Boston, Lincolnshire PE21 9HZ. Tel: (01205) 365501. Producers of excellent quality tractor fed and other labels.

Viking Direct, Bursom Industrial Park, Tollwell Road, Leicester LE4 1BR. Tel: 0800 424444. Mail order suppliers of office stationery and other supplies.

Further Reading

How to Do Your Own Advertising, Michael Bennie (How To Books Ltd, 1990). An excellent introduction to effective advertising, covering layout, copywriting, and targeting.

Decent Exposure, Vincent Yearley (Kogan Page). A good introduction to obtaining publicity generally – includes a useful section on producing press releases.

The Craft of Copywriting, Alastair Crompton (Business Books). A very useful book which concentrates on the production of effective copy for ads.

How to Write a Press Release, Peter Bartram (How To Books Ltd, 2nd edition 1995). An excellent guide from one of Britain's most published business writers.

The Designer's Handbook, Alistair Campbell (MacDonald, 1983). The design 'bible', still much used in spite of its age.

How to Write a CV That Works, Paul McGee (How To Books, 1995). A very comprehensive guide, dealing with a variety of approaches.

How to Master Book-Keeping, Peter Marshall (How To Books, 2nd edition, 1995). Aimed at students of the subject, very comprehensive and easy to follow.

Book-Keeping and Accounts, Geoffrey Whitehead (Natwest Business Handbooks Pitman). Aimed at the small trader, and especially valuable to beginners in the subject.

How to Use the Internet, Graham Jones (How To Books, 1996). A real beginners's guide.

How to Write & Sell Computer Software, Stephen Harding (How To Books, 1996). Explains how to break into the huge and lucrative market for business, games and other types of software.

Buying a Personal Computer, Allen Brown (How To Books, 1996). Everything you need to know without sinking into a sea of jargon.

Index

How To Books

How To Books provide practical help on a large range of topics. They are available through all good bookshops or can be ordered direct from the distributors. Just tick the titles you want and complete the form on the following page.

___ Apply to an Industrial Tribunal (£7.99)
___ Applying for a Job (£7.99)
___ Applying for a United States Visa (£15.99)
___ Be a Freelance Journalist (£8.99)
___ Be a Freelance Secretary (£8.99)
___ Be a Local Councillor (£8.99)
___ Be an Effective School Governor (£9.99)
___ Become a Freelance Sales Agent (£9.99)
___ Become an Au Pair (£8.99)
___ Buy & Run a Shop (£8.99)
___ Buy & Run a Small Hotel (£8.99)
___ Cash from your Computer (£9.99)
___ Career Planning for Women (£8.99)
___ Choosing a Nursing Home (£8.99)
___ Claim State Benefits (£9.99)
___ Communicate at Work (£7.99)
___ Conduct Staff Appraisals (£7.99)
___ Conducting Effective Interviews (£8.99)
___ Copyright & Law for Writers (£8.99)
___ Counsel People at Work (£7.99)
___ Creating a Twist in the Tale (£8.99)
___ Creative Writing (£9.99)
___ Critical Thinking for Students (£8.99)
___ Do Voluntary Work Abroad (£8.99)
___ Do Your Own Advertising (£8.99)
___ Do Your Own PR (£8.99)
___ Doing Business Abroad (£9.99)
___ Emigrate (£9.99)
___ Employ & Manage Staff (£8.99)
___ Find Temporary Work Abroad (£8.99)
___ Finding a Job in Canada (£9.99)
___ Finding a Job in Computers (£8.99)
___ Finding a Job in New Zealand (£9.99)
___ Finding a Job with a Future (£8.99)
___ Finding Work Overseas (£9.99)
___ Freelance DJ-ing (£8.99)
___ Get a Job Abroad (£10.99)
___ Get a Job in America (£9.99)
___ Get a Job in Australia (£9.99)
___ Get a Job in Europe (£9.99)
___ Get a Job in France (£9.99)
___ Get a Job in Germany (£9.99)
___ Get a Job in Hotels and Catering (£8.99)
___ Get a Job in Travel & Tourism (£8.99)
___ Get into Films & TV (£8.99)
___ Get into Radio (£8.99)
___ Get That Job (£6.99)
___ Getting your First Job (£8.99)
___ Going to University (£8.99)
___ Helping your Child to Read (£8.99)
___ Investing in People (£8.99)
___ Invest in Stocks & Shares (£8.99)

___ Keep Business Accounts (£7.99)
___ Know Your Rights at Work (£8.99)
___ Know Your Rights: Teachers (£6.99)
___ Live & Work in America (£9.99)
___ Live & Work in Australia (£12.99)
___ Live & Work in Germany (£9.99)
___ Live & Work in Greece (£9.99)
___ Live & Work in Italy (£8.99)
___ Live & Work in New Zealand (£9.99)
___ Live & Work in Portugal (£9.99)
___ Live & Work in Spain (£7.99)
___ Live & Work in the Gulf (£9.99)
___ Living & Working in Britain (£8.99)
___ Living & Working in China (£9.99)
___ Living & Working in Hong Kong (£10.99)
___ Living & Working in Israel (£10.99)
___ Living & Working in Japan (£8.99)
___ Living & Working in Saudi Arabia (£12.99)
___ Living & Working in the Netherlands (£9.99)
___ Lose Weight & Keep Fit (£6.99)
___ Make a Wedding Speech (£7.99)
___ Making a Complaint (£8.99)
___ Manage a Sales Team (£8.99)
___ Manage an Office (£8.99)
___ Manage Computers at Work (£8.99)
___ Manage People at Work (£8.99)
___ Manage Your Career (£8.99)
___ Managing Budgets & Cash Flows (£9.99)
___ Managing Meetings (£8.99)
___ Managing Your Personal Finances (£8.99)
___ Market Yourself (£8.99)
___ Master Book-Keeping (£8.99)
___ Mastering Business English (£8.99)
___ Master GCSE Accounts (£8.99)
___ Master Languages (£8.99)
___ Master Public Speaking (£8.99)
___ Obtaining Visas & Work Permits (£9.99)
___ Organising Effective Training (£9.99)
___ Pass Exams Without Anxiety (£7.99)
___ Pass That Interview (£6.99)
___ Plan a Wedding (£7.99)
___ Prepare a Business Plan (£8.99)
___ Publish a Book (£9.99)
___ Publish a Newsletter (£9.99)
___ Raise Funds & Sponsorship (£7.99)
___ Rent & Buy Property in France (£9.99)
___ Rent & Buy Property in Italy (£9.99)
___ Retire Abroad (£8.99)
___ Return to Work (£7.99)
___ Run a Local Campaign (£6.99)
___ Run a Voluntary Group (£8.99)
___ Sell Your Business (£9.99)

How To Books

___ Selling into Japan (£14.99)
___ Setting up Home in Florida (£9.99)
___ Spend a Year Abroad (£8.99)
___ Start a Business from Home (£7.99)
___ Start a New Career (£6.99)
___ Starting to Manage (£8.99)
___ Starting to Write (£8.99)
___ Start Word Processing (£8.99)
___ Start Your Own Business (£8.99)
___ Study Abroad (£8.99)
___ Study & Learn (£7.99)
___ Study & Live in Britain (£7.99)
___ Studying at University (£8.99)
___ Studying for a Degree (£8.99)
___ Successful Grandparenting (£8.99)
___ Successful Mail Order Marketing (£9.99)
___ Successful Single Parenting (£8.99)
___ Survive at College (£4.99)
___ Survive Divorce (£8.99)
___ Surviving Redundancy (£8.99)
___ Take Care of Your Heart (£5.99)
___ Taking in Students (£8.99)
___ Taking on Staff (£8.99)
___ Taking Your A-Levels (£8.99)
___ Teach Abroad (£8.99)
___ Teach Adults (£8.99)
___ Teaching Someone to Drive (£8.99)
___ Travel Round the World (£8.99)
___ Use a Library (£6.99)

___ Use the Internet (£9.99)
___ Winning Consumer Competitions (£8.99)
___ Winning Presentations (£8.99)
___ Work from Home (£8.99)
___ Work in an Office (£7.99)
___ Work in Retail (£8.99)
___ Work with Dogs (£8.99)
___ Working Abroad (£14.99)
___ Working as a Holiday Rep (£9.99)
___ Working in Japan (£10.99)
___ Working in Photography (£8.99)
___ Working in the Gulf (£10.99)
___ Working on Contract Worldwide (£9.99)
___ Working on Cruise Ships (£9.99)
___ Write a CV that Works (£7.99)
___ Write a Press Release (£9.99)
___ Write a Report (£8.99)
___ Write an Assignment (£8.99)
___ Write an Essay (£7.99)
___ Write & Sell Computer Software (£9.99)
___ Write Business Letters (£8.99)
___ Write for Publication (£8.99)
___ Write for Television (£8.99)
___ Write Your Dissertation (£8.99)
___ Writing a Non Fiction Book (£8.99)
___ Writing & Selling a Novel (£8.99)
___ Writing & Selling Short Stories (£8.99)
___ Writing Reviews (£8.99)
___ Your Own Business in Europe (£12.99)

To: Plymbridge Distributors Ltd, Plymbridge House, Estover Road, Plymouth PL6 7PZ.
Customer Services Tel: (01752) 202301. Fax: (01752) 202331.

Please send me copies of the titles I have indicated. Please add postage & packing (UK £1, Europe including Eire, £2, World £3 airmail).

☐ I enclose cheque/PO payable to Plymbridge Distributors Ltd for £

☐ Please charge to my ☐ MasterCard, ☐ Visa, ☐ AMEX card.

Account No. [ ][ ][ ][ ][ ][ ][ ][ ][ ][ ][ ][ ][ ][ ][ ][ ]

Card Expiry Date [ ][ ] 19   ☎ **Credit Card orders may be faxed or phoned.**

Customer Name (CAPITALS) ....

Address ....

.... Postcode ....

Telephone .... Signature ....

Every effort will be made to despatch your copy as soon as possible but to avoid possible disappointment please allow up to 21 days for despatch time (42 days if overseas). Prices and availability are subject to change without notice.

Code BPA